THE PSYCHOLOGY OF SAFETY

Understanding Human Behavior Before Failure Occurs

Volume I of the Professional Safety Leadership Series

By James Dye

Safety Professional | Military Veteran | Operational Safety Leader

2026 Edition

COPYRIGHT

Published by Dye Safety Publishing.

This book is intended for leadership development, safety education, and operational improvement. It is not a substitute for legal, regulatory, medical, clinical, or professional judgment. It does not provide diagnosis, treatment, counseling, legal advice, or regulatory interpretation. For mental health concerns, medical concerns, legal guidance, or regulatory interpretation, consult a qualified professional or the appropriate authority.

ISBN (Paperback): To be assigned
ISBN (eBook): To be assigned
Printed in the United States of America

DEDICATION

This volume is dedicated to Donna Osborne, whose professional journey and commitment to safety leadership helped inspire the development of this work.

Donna's career reflects the value of growth through experience, dedication, and service. Beginning in manufacturing at the entry level and advancing to a frontline supervisory role over seventeen years, she demonstrated what it means to lead from where you stand.

She later devoted twenty years to public service in the safety profession, progressing from Safety Officer to Safety Manager. Her passion for protecting people — not through compliance alone, but through genuine care and sustained attention — is the spirit this series was written to honor.

THE PROFESSIONAL SAFETY LEADERSHIP SERIES

Volume I — The Psychology of Safety

The anchor book. Explores why capable people make dangerous decisions and what leaders can do before failure occurs.

Volume II — Coaching for Safety Leadership

Practical coaching tools for supervisors and safety professionals who develop safety thinking in others.

Volume III — Before the Incident: Using the 5 How's Before the 5 Why's

The 5 How's preventive analysis framework applied to pre-task planning and field leadership.

Volume IV — The 5 How's and 5 Why's Safety Leadership Handbook

A complete field reference integrating preventive and investigative analysis for daily leadership use.

Volume V — Safety & Finance

A leadership-focused look at the financial impact of safety decisions, prevention, and operational risk.

Volume VI — Safety Leadership in the Field

A practical field leadership volume focused on applying safety leadership principles during daily operations.

TABLE OF CONTENTS

INTRODUCTION

Safety is often discussed in terms of procedures, equipment, training records, inspections, and regulatory compliance. Those elements matter. A workplace cannot build a strong safety culture without consistent standards, reliable controls, and clear expectations. But procedures and equipment do not make decisions. People do.

Most employees do not come to work intending to get hurt or to place others at risk. In many serious incidents, the people involved are capable, experienced, and hardworking. They are not trying to fail. They are responding — rationally, from inside their own experience — to conditions that their work environment has taught them are acceptable. Understanding how that happens is the purpose of this book.

This is not a clinical mental health guide. It does not diagnose or treat mental illness. Its focus is occupational safety psychology: the way human performance, stress, fatigue, communication, group dynamics, and leadership behavior interact to either prevent or contribute to workplace incidents. It is written for the field — for the supervisors, safety professionals, and operational leaders who work with real crews in real conditions.

The strongest safety cultures do not wait until someone is injured to start asking better questions. They ask how exposure is developing now. They look for weak signals. They notice when communication is compressing, when familiar hazards are stopping to register, when pressure is shortening the space that careful thinking requires. They understand that the moment of injury is the end of a long process — and that the real opportunity is in the middle of that process, before it concludes.

This volume is the anchor of the Professional Safety Leadership Series. Every other volume builds on what is established here: that safety is not primarily a compliance problem, a training problem, or an equipment problem. It is a human performance problem that requires leaders who understand what is happening inside people before anything goes wrong.

How to Use This Book

This book is designed for frontline supervisors, safety professionals, project leaders, managers, executives, and anyone responsible for influencing behavior in operational environments. It can be used for individual study, team development, supervisor coaching, or organizational safety culture improvement.

Each chapter follows a consistent structure: the leadership issue, the psychology behind it, a field example, what the operational mechanism looks like, what leaders should look for, how to apply the concept, how to develop it in others, how to integrate it in daily operations, key leadership questions, common field traps, prevention practices, connection to the 5 How's framework, a toolbox talk prompt, a chapter summary, and a leader action checklist.

Do not try to implement everything at once. Select one chapter, connect it to something real in your current work environment, and practice the specific behaviors it recommends. The most effective learning from this volume comes from application — not from reading alone.

PART I — THE HUMAN SIDE OF RISK

Understanding why incidents happen requires looking past the final act. Part I examines the psychological forces that shape human behavior in operational environments — how the brain adapts to risk, how pressure changes decisions, and how exposure grows long before anyone recognizes it.

Chapter 1

WHY GOOD PEOPLE MAKE DANGEROUS DECISIONS

Leadership Issue

Leaders often focus on the outcome of a decision rather than the conditions that shaped it. When a capable, experienced employee is involved in an incident, the natural question is 'why didn't they know better?' But this question leads to the wrong answer. The more useful question is: what did the work environment teach this person was acceptable? Capable employees make dangerous decisions when pressure, familiarity, incomplete information, and system conditions make risk feel reasonable in the moment. Understanding that mechanism is the first step toward preventing it.

The Psychology Behind the Risk

James Reason's work on organizational accidents established that incidents are rarely caused by a single act of carelessness. They develop through layers of latent conditions — organizational decisions, resource constraints, management pressures, and system weaknesses — that align to create the opportunity for failure. Sidney Dekker extended this thinking by showing that workers' behavior makes sense from inside the context they were operating in. They were not ignoring safety; they were responding rationally to the signals their environment was sending them.

One of the most damaging errors in post-incident analysis is hindsight bias. Once an outcome is known, the path to it appears obvious. Leaders look back and believe the hazard was clearly visible, the warning signs were unmistakable, and the safe choice was easy. None of that was true at the time. The employees involved were making decisions with incomplete information, under time constraints, in a system that had normalized certain shortcuts. Judging those decisions by their outcome rather than by the conditions that existed at the time produces blame instead of learning.

Field Example

A skilled mechanic removes a guard for a brief adjustment because the machine has been down for an hour and the crew is waiting. The decision is not made because the mechanic does not care about safety; it is made because experience, urgency, and previous success create a context where the action feels reasonable. The guard comes off dozens of times without incident. This time, it does not.

Operational Mechanism

The mechanism at work in this chapter is the interaction between system conditions and individual perception. Employees do not make decisions in isolation. They respond to signals from their environment: how long pauses are tolerated, how often procedures are verified, whether previous shortcuts produced consequences, and what leadership rewards or ignores. A worker who skips a step is not simply being careless — they are acting in a system that has taught them that skipping that step is acceptable. The decision feels reasonable because the environment has made it feel reasonable.

What Leaders Should Look For

- Employees explaining their decisions by referencing what 'always works' rather than what the procedure requires.

- A gap between written expectations and observed field practice that has existed long enough to feel normal.
- Workers who hesitate before a task but proceed anyway without voicing their concern.
- Supervisors accepting small deviations from standards because the work is moving and no harm has occurred.
- Post-incident language that focuses on the individual's mistake without examining what the system contributed.

Leadership Application

The leader's role is to examine conditions, not just behaviors. When an unsafe act occurs, the first question should not be 'who did this?' but 'what made this feel like the right thing to do?' That shift in framing opens the conversation toward system improvement rather than individual blame. It also sends a signal to the workforce that reporting concerns and near-misses is safe — because the response will be learning, not punishment.

This does not eliminate accountability. When someone knowingly ignores a standard, accountability is appropriate and necessary. The distinction is between an employee who made a reasonable decision in a flawed system and one who recklessly disregarded a standard they understood. Strong leaders apply accountability precisely and learning broadly. Most incidents call for more learning and less punishment than organizations typically deliver.

Leadership Development Focus

Supervisors need to develop two distinct capabilities that are sometimes in tension: the ability to hold people accountable to standards, and the ability to investigate conditions that shaped behavior. Both are necessary. A supervisor who only enforces rules without examining conditions will miss the systemic issues that produce repeated incidents. A supervisor who only examines conditions without enforcing standards will allow gradual degradation of safety discipline.

The development target is a leader who can hold both simultaneously — who says 'this standard was not followed, and we need to understand why' rather than choosing one or the other. This requires practice, coaching, and organizational support for the learning approach.

Practical Field Integration

Integrate this concept by adding one question to your existing pre-task and post-task routines: 'What conditions could make an unsafe decision feel reasonable here?' Ask it before high-risk work as a way to surface latent issues. Ask it after a near-miss or unsafe act as a way to move the conversation beyond blame.

Over time, this question builds a habit of condition-focused thinking across the team. Employees begin asking it themselves, which is the real goal. When crews habitually examine what makes risk feel reasonable, they catch drift before it produces incidents.

Leadership Questions

- What conditions in this work environment make the unsafe option feel easier or more reasonable than the safe option?
- If I were this employee, working under these pressures and with this experience, would this decision have made sense to me?
- What has our system — scheduling, resourcing, communication, leadership behavior — taught people about what is actually acceptable?
- What have we tolerated, normalized, or failed to correct that contributed to this outcome?
- What would make the safe choice easier, faster, or more natural than the unsafe choice in this context?

Common Field Traps

- Focusing on the individual's decision without examining the system conditions that shaped it — this produces blame without learning.

- Using hindsight to make the unsafe decision look obviously wrong, which prevents honest analysis of how it felt reasonable at the time.
- Assuming that experienced workers automatically make safer decisions — experience can increase confidence without increasing awareness of gradual drift.
- Treating incident investigations as legal or HR processes rather than learning opportunities, which suppresses honest reporting.
- Assuming that posting a rule or adding a form will change behavior without addressing the underlying conditions that drive the behavior.

Prevention Practices

- Before any non-routine task, pause and ask what conditions in this situation could make an unsafe choice feel acceptable.
- After any near-miss or unsafe act, conduct a conditions review before drawing conclusions about individual responsibility.
- Track the gap between written procedures and observed field practice — this gap is where dangerous decisions develop.
- Create a standing expectation that employees can voice concerns about conditions without fear of retaliation or dismissal.
- Use repeat incidents as evidence of system conditions, not individual failure — patterns indicate systemic issues that single accountability cannot fix.

Connection to the 5 How's

The 5 How's directly address the conditions this chapter describes. 'How can this task fail?' forces leaders to examine the system conditions that could produce a dangerous decision before work begins. 'How will failure be prevented?' moves the conversation toward controls rather than blame. Used consistently, the 5 How's build exactly the habit of condition-focused thinking that prevents capable people from making dangerous decisions.

Supervisor Toolbox Talk Prompt

Use this prompt with your crew: 'Before we start, I want to ask: what conditions in this task today could make an unsafe choice feel like the right call? What would pressure us to skip a step or take a shortcut?' Let the crew answer first. What comes up in that conversation tells you more about actual risk than any inspection form.

Chapter Summary

- Capable, experienced employees make dangerous decisions when system conditions — pressure, familiarity, silence, incomplete information — make risk feel reasonable in the moment.
- Hindsight bias causes leaders to overestimate how obvious the safe choice was, which prevents honest learning from incidents.
- The most useful post-incident question is not 'why didn't they know better?' but 'what did our system teach them was acceptable?'
- Prevention improves when leaders examine conditions, not just behaviors — and when they make the safe choice easier than the unsafe choice.

Leader Action Checklist

[ ] Identify one work condition this week that could make an unsafe decision feel reasonable to your crew.

[ ] Review a recent correction and ask whether the underlying system condition was actually addressed.

[ ] Ask one crew member what conditions in their work make it difficult to follow the procedure exactly.

[ ] Examine one gap between written procedure and actual field practice and decide whether the procedure or the practice needs to change.

Chapter 2

THE BRAIN AND RISK NORMALIZATION

Leadership Issue

The brain is designed to adapt. When people are exposed to the same hazard repeatedly without experiencing harm, the brain reduces its alarm response to that hazard. What once triggered caution becomes routine. What once seemed dangerous becomes ordinary. This process — called habituation — is a normal cognitive function that allows people to work efficiently in complex environments. But in safety, it is one of the most dangerous forces a leader will face, because the hazard does not change when the alarm response does.

The Psychology Behind the Risk

Reason (1997) described how people develop 'rules-based' behavior through repeated exposure — mental shortcuts that allow experienced workers to navigate complex tasks without deliberate analysis of every step. These shortcuts are efficient and necessary. They become dangerous when the conditions they were built for change and the shortcuts remain. Hollnagel (2014) extended this with his FRAM model, showing that performance variability is normal and that safety depends on managing the conditions under which variability occurs, not eliminating human adaptability.

Neuroscience offers a direct explanation. The brain's reticular activating system filters sensory input based on novelty and perceived importance. Stimuli that appear repeatedly without producing a meaningful outcome are progressively downgraded. A warning sign that the crew passes every day eventually registers no differently than a wall. This is not negligence — it is how the brain conserves cognitive resources. Leaders cannot prevent habituation from occurring. They can, however, create conditions that interrupt it before it produces exposure.

Field Example

A crew walks past open equipment travel paths every day. At first they keep clear distance. After months without a close call, they begin crossing casually because the hazard has become visually ordinary. The equipment has not slowed down. The risk has not changed. But the crew's perceptual response to it has faded to the point where it no longer triggers protective behavior.

Operational Mechanism

Normalization operates through repetition and outcome. Every time a worker is exposed to a hazard and nothing happens, the brain updates its prediction: this hazard does not produce harm. Over time, this prediction becomes strong enough to override the original training-based response. The process accelerates when leadership behavior confirms it — when supervisors walk past the same conditions without comment, the message received is that the conditions are acceptable. What leaders ignore, they teach.

What Leaders Should Look For

- Experienced workers moving through established hazard zones with no observable pause, scan, or positioning adjustment.
- Crew members who cannot articulate the current hazard controls when asked — they know the task but not the protection.
- Warning signs, barriers, or posted reminders that receive no attention from workers who pass them daily.
- New employees adopting unsafe behaviors within their first few weeks because the crew models them as normal.
- Safety walk-throughs that identify the same conditions repeatedly without producing sustained correction.

Leadership Application

The most effective tool against normalization is deliberate re-sensitization — structured opportunities that force the brain to process a familiar hazard as if seeing it for the first time. This can be as simple as asking a new employee to describe their observations during a safety walk, then comparing what they see to what experienced workers notice. The gaps in that comparison reveal exactly where normalization has occurred.

Another effective approach is the 'fresh eyes' request: ask someone unfamiliar with the work area to walk it with you and point out anything that would concern them. This person's observations are a direct window into what habituation has made invisible to the regular crew. Leaders should act visibly on what is found — not as punishment, but as confirmation that fresh observations are valuable and acted upon.

Leadership Development Focus

Supervisors need to understand that normalization affects them just as much as their crews. A supervisor who has managed the same work area for three years may have normalized the same hazards their crew has. This makes self-awareness an essential leadership skill — the ability to ask 'have I stopped seeing this because it stopped being dangerous, or because I've been looking at it too long?'

Supervisor development should include regular rotation of safety observation responsibilities, deliberate exposure to outside perspectives, and structured comparison of current conditions to documented baseline expectations. Leaders who never compare their current field reality to written standards miss the gradual drift that normalization produces.

Practical Field Integration

Build re-sensitization into your regular rhythm. On a monthly basis, identify one hazard that has been present for more than 90 days and conduct a deliberate re-evaluation: is the current control still adequate? Have conditions around it changed? Does the crew still treat it with appropriate awareness? This is not an audit — it is a deliberate interruption of normalization.

Also use personnel transitions as re-sensitization opportunities. When a new employee joins the crew, ask them within their first two weeks what concerns them about the work environment. Their answers will tell you what the rest of the crew has stopped seeing. Treat their observations as valuable intelligence, not naïve overcaution.

Leadership Questions

- When did this crew stop treating this hazard as genuinely dangerous, and what changed — the hazard or their perception of it?
- What would a new employee with no prior exposure to this work area identify as concerning in the first 30 minutes?
- Which hazards in this environment have not produced an incident in so long that the crew may have stopped believing they can?
- What warning signs, barriers, or posted controls has this crew learned to walk past without reading?
- Have I, as the leader, normalized conditions in this area that I would flag immediately if I saw them somewhere else?

Common Field Traps

- Interpreting crew confidence around a known hazard as competence — familiarity and competence are not the same, and in some cases they move in opposite directions.
- Assuming that because the crew has worked this hazard safely for years, their current approach is still adequate.
- Relying on posted warnings and training records as evidence that normalization has not occurred — these are inputs, not outcomes.
- Failing to act on new-employee observations because experienced workers dismiss them as overcaution.
- Measuring safety performance by lagging indicators (injuries) rather than leading indicators (habituation signals) — by the time an injury occurs, normalization has been established for months.

Prevention Practices

- Schedule quarterly 'fresh eyes' reviews of your most familiar work areas — bring in someone who does not work there regularly and ask what they notice.
- Periodically ask crew members to describe the current hazard controls in their area; inability to answer is an early normalization signal.
- Rotate safety observation responsibilities so no supervisor is evaluating only areas they manage — familiarity reduces observation quality.
- Use near-miss events as normalization alerts: if something almost happened in an area the crew considers routine, normalization has occurred.
- Create a standing practice of comparing current field conditions to baseline documented expectations at least twice per year.

Connection to the 5 How's

The 5 How's interrupt normalization by forcing deliberate thinking before each task. 'How can this task fail?' cannot be answered honestly by a crew that has stopped seeing the hazards. When leaders use this question consistently — especially for tasks the crew considers routine — they rebuild the cognitive engagement that normalization has eroded.

Supervisor Toolbox Talk Prompt

Try this with your crew: 'I want everyone to look at this area like you've never seen it before. Pretend it's your first day. What would concern you?' Give people a moment to actually look, then listen. You will hear things that don't come up in normal safety conversations — and some of those things will matter.

Chapter Summary

- Habituation is a normal brain function that progressively reduces the alarm response to hazards that have not recently produced harm — the hazard does not become safer, only more familiar.

- Normalization is reinforced when leadership walks past the same conditions without comment, teaching the crew that those conditions are acceptable.
- The most effective tool against normalization is deliberate re-sensitization: structured opportunities to process familiar hazards with fresh cognitive engagement.
- New employees and outside observers are among the most valuable safety resources available — they see what normalization has made invisible to the regular crew.

Leader Action Checklist

[ ] Identify the three hazards in your work area that the crew has been exposed to the longest and evaluate whether current awareness of them is adequate.

[ ] Ask a new employee or someone unfamiliar with your area to share what they notice — and document what they say.

[ ] Find one warning sign or barrier that workers pass daily and verify that the crew can explain what it is protecting against.

[ ] Compare current field conditions in one area to the baseline documented expectations and identify any gaps.

Chapter 3

WHY FAMILIAR HAZARDS STOP FEELING DANGEROUS

Leadership Issue

There is an important difference between a hazard that workers know about and a hazard that workers respond to. Experienced crews often know every hazard in their environment — they can list them, describe them, and explain the controls. But knowing about a hazard and feeling its danger are different cognitive states. Familiarity erodes the emotional signal that drives protective behavior. A worker who knows about a fall hazard and a worker who feels its danger will behave differently. The goal of safety leadership is not just knowledge — it is sustained, appropriate behavioral response.

The Psychology Behind the Risk

Perceptual adaptation is the brain's tendency to reduce its response to stimuli that are constant or predictable. In visual processing, this is why we stop noticing background sounds or the feeling of our own clothing. In safety, it is why a worker who has been on scaffolding every day for two years no longer feels the instinctive caution that a new employee feels on their first day at height. The emotional signal that once produced careful, deliberate behavior has faded — replaced by a procedural response that is often faster and less attentive.

Research on high-reliability organizations (Weick & Sutcliffe, 2001) identifies 'preoccupation with failure' as a core characteristic of safe, high-performing teams. These teams do not allow familiarity to lower vigilance — they maintain an active mental model of what can go wrong even in routine operations. This is not natural; it requires deliberate cultivation. Leaders who understand perceptual adaptation can build practices that sustain it.

Field Example

Workers who were once cautious around elevated work begin treating the edge, lift, or scaffold as routine. The height has not changed, but the emotional reaction to it has faded. Pre-task setup — which used to be careful and deliberate — is now done quickly, with less checking, because it has been done the same way hundreds of times without a problem.

Operational Mechanism

The mechanism is emotional habituation combined with procedural confidence. As a task is repeated, emotional engagement decreases and procedural speed increases. This feels like mastery, and in many ways it is — the worker genuinely has learned the task. But procedural speed without emotional engagement removes the signal that triggers pause-and-verify behavior. When something unusual happens within a familiar task — a change in conditions, a new variable — the worker's procedural mode may not slow down fast enough to catch it.

What Leaders Should Look For

- Experienced workers completing pre-task setups significantly faster than the written procedure allows, often skipping verification steps.
- Crew members who express mild irritation or impatience when asked to slow down or verify a familiar task.
- A task that used to prompt questions and discussion that now begins with no apparent planning conversation.
- Workers who cannot identify what has changed in a task environment because they stopped actively scanning it.
- Protective equipment being worn correctly at the start of a shift but incorrectly by mid-task because adjustment feels unnecessary.

Leadership Application

The goal is not to make experienced workers feel like novices — that approach is patronizing and counterproductive. The goal is to sustain appropriate engagement with the task's actual risk level, regardless of how familiar it has become. One way to do this is to separate familiarity from verification: acknowledge that the crew knows this task well, then ask them to verify current conditions anyway. Frame it as protecting against what changes, not against what is always the same.

When workers push back on verification for familiar tasks, that pushback is itself a signal. 'We always do it this way' and 'we've done this a hundred times' are phrases that indicate familiarity-based confidence has overtaken current-conditions awareness. These are coaching moments, not compliance moments.

Leadership Development Focus

Supervisors need to develop the ability to distinguish between competence-based speed and familiarity-based shortcuts. Both look the same from the outside — the task is completed quickly — but they come from different places. Competence-based speed includes ongoing situational scanning; familiarity-based shortcuts involve running a procedural script without updating it against current conditions.

One development practice that helps supervisors develop this skill is watching experienced workers complete familiar tasks and asking: 'At what points in that task did they pause and scan versus run on autopilot?' Identifying those moments builds the supervisor's ability to see where familiarity has replaced awareness.

Practical Field Integration

Introduce the concept of the 'familiarity check' — a brief pause before any task the crew has done more than 50 times — that asks one question: 'What is different about the conditions today compared to when we did this last?' This question cannot be answered from memory. It requires looking. It takes ten seconds and reactivates the situational scanning that familiarity suppresses.

Post this question at task start points for your highest-frequency work. Make it a standing expectation, not a special event. Over time, the crew begins asking it automatically — which is the goal.

Leadership Questions

- For the tasks this crew does most frequently, when did they last approach them with the same level of attention they gave them the first time?
- What would change about how this task is performed if no one in the crew had ever done it before?
- At what point in this task does procedural confidence replace active situational awareness?
- What is genuinely different about conditions today versus the last time this task was performed — and has the crew noticed?
- What hazards in this environment have the crew stopped reacting to physically, even though they would describe them as dangerous if asked?

Common Field Traps

- Interpreting smooth, fast task completion as evidence that conditions are well-managed — speed often indicates habituation, not safety.
- Accepting 'we've always done it this way' as a justification for skipping verification — this phrase is a warning sign, not a reassurance.
- Assuming that a crew's ability to describe a hazard means they are actively managing their response to it.
- Scheduling safety observations only for high-risk or non-routine tasks — the most dangerous normalization is happening in the familiar, routine ones.
- Using training completion records to conclude that hazard awareness is maintained — training awareness and field awareness are not the same thing after 100 repetitions.

Prevention Practices

- Implement a standing 'familiarity check' before any task the crew performs more than twice per week — one question about what has changed today.
- Periodically assign a 'slow walk' to a familiar task: perform it at half the normal pace and notice every step that is normally done automatically.
- Use new employees' early observations as a calibration tool — compare what they flag to what experienced workers no longer notice.
- For your highest-frequency tasks, review whether the pre-task verification steps are actually being completed or being assumed.
- Create specific re-engagement triggers for tasks where familiarity is highest — personnel changes, seasonal shifts, or equipment modifications that require treating the task as relatively new.

Connection to the 5 How's

The 5 How's are most powerful when applied to the tasks a crew considers most routine. 'How can this task fail?' is rarely asked about familiar tasks — which is exactly where the answer is most needed. Building the habit of applying the 5 How's to routine work is the most effective antidote to familiarity-based complacency.

Supervisor Toolbox Talk Prompt

Ask your crew: 'Pick the task you do most often — the one you could do in your sleep. Now tell me: what would have to be different today for that task to go wrong?' If the conversation is quick and dismissive, that is your signal. If it opens up genuine discussion about conditions, you are where you want to be.

Chapter Summary

- Familiarity reduces the emotional signal that drives protective behavior — experienced workers often know about hazards but no longer feel them as dangerous.

- Perceptual adaptation is normal and cannot be prevented; the leader's job is to build practices that interrupt it before it erodes protective behavior.
- Competence-based speed and familiarity-based shortcuts look identical from the outside — distinguishing them requires watching where workers scan versus where they run on autopilot.
- The most valuable safety observations happen during the crew's most familiar, most routine tasks — that is where dangerous normalization is most advanced.

Leader Action Checklist

[ ] Identify the two tasks your crew performs most frequently and evaluate whether pre-task verification is actually occurring or being assumed.

[ ] Observe one familiar task this week and note specifically where the crew stops scanning and starts running on procedural autopilot.

[ ] Introduce the 'familiarity check' question to one high-frequency task and document what the crew identifies as having changed.

[ ] Ask one experienced worker to describe a familiar hazard and then ask how they behave around it — compare the two answers.

Chapter 4

PRESSURE CHANGES HUMAN BEHAVIOR

Leadership Issue

Pressure is one of the most consistent contributors to unsafe behavior, yet it is also one of the most overlooked. Most safety systems focus on physical hazards, procedural compliance, and equipment controls. Very few systematically examine the effect of schedule pressure, production demands, and social pressure on the decisions workers make moment to moment. Pressure does not eliminate a person's knowledge of the safe procedure. It changes the relative weight of competing priorities – making speed feel more urgent than verification, making completion feel more important than caution.

The Psychology Behind the Risk

Research in behavioral economics and organizational psychology consistently shows that time pressure narrows attention, increases risk tolerance, and reduces the quality of decision-making. Reason (1990) identified production pressure as one of the primary latent conditions in organizational accidents – not because organizations intend to trade safety for production, but because the signals they send workers every day create exactly that trade-off implicitly. When a supervisor checks schedule status five times per shift and safety status once per week, the workforce receives a clear message about what matters most.

Social pressure operates differently but with similar effect. Workers who slow down for safety in an environment where everyone else is moving fast experience social costs: being seen as slow, difficult, or uncommitted. Milgram's conformity research and later work on workplace voice suppression both show that social pressure from peers and authority figures can override an individual's private judgment, even when that judgment is correct.

Field Example

A supervisor tells the crew to work safely, but body language, impatience, and repeated comments about schedule send a stronger message: hurry up. The crew shortens planning without being directly told to do so. Verification steps are assumed rather than completed. The work moves faster, and everyone interprets the faster pace as compliance with the supervisor's real expectation — not the stated one.

Operational Mechanism

The mechanism is dual-signal conflict. Leaders send explicit signals (the policy, the statement, the posted rule) and implicit signals (behavior, attention, reaction, questions asked). When these signals conflict, implicit signals consistently win. A workforce that hears 'safety is first' but sees schedule reviewed at every meeting and safety reviewed quarterly does not believe safety is first. They believe what they observe. Every behavior a leader engages in teaches the crew what actually matters.

What Leaders Should Look For

- Pre-task planning conversations getting shorter or disappearing entirely as deadline pressure increases.
- Workers using shorthand or assumption-based communication ('same as yesterday,' 'you know what to do') during high-tempo periods.
- Concerns being raised and then withdrawn quickly when the crew reads the supervisor's body language as impatient.
- Verification steps being completed on paper but not observed in the field — documentation running ahead of actual task execution.
- The pace of the work accelerating after a delay without anyone explicitly discussing whether the plan still fits the new timeline.

Leadership Application

Leaders must audit their own implicit signals before they can address pressure-driven behavior in their crews. The questions to ask are: What do I check on most often? What gets my immediate attention and what waits? What do I visibly react to with urgency? Workers watch leaders more carefully than leaders realize, and they adjust their behavior to match what they observe, not what they are told.

The most powerful signal a leader can send against production pressure is the visible, unhurried pause. When a leader stops a task for a verification without apology, without visible frustration, and without a rush to resume — that behavior teaches the crew that pausing is genuinely acceptable. It is a more effective safety message than any posted policy.

Leadership Development Focus

Supervisors need to develop awareness of their own behavioral signals under pressure. Most supervisors who create unsafe pressure in their crews are not doing so intentionally — they are managing real schedule demands while simultaneously trying to meet safety expectations. The problem is that under pressure, people default to the priority that has historically produced the most immediate consequences, and in most organizations, that is production.

Development should include practice with pressure-response scenarios: when the schedule is three hours behind and the crew is asking for direction, what does the supervisor say, how do they say it, and what do they check first? Rehearsing these moments before they occur gives supervisors a response pattern that doesn't default to the production-first habit under stress.

Practical Field Integration

Create a standing 'pressure audit' for your highest-tempo periods. Before a push or a deadline, identify which safety verification steps are most likely to be compressed or skipped under pressure and put a specific countermeasure in place for each one. This is not about creating more paperwork — it is about identifying in advance where pressure will find the path of least resistance and blocking it.

After high-tempo periods, conduct a brief review: what safety practices were compromised, what was skipped, what was assumed? Normalize this review as a standard part of project completion, not a fault-finding exercise.

Leadership Questions

- What implicit signals am I sending about the relative priority of schedule and safety — not what I say, but what I check, react to, and visibly care about?
- During the last high-pressure period, what safety verification steps were completed fully and which were assumed or abbreviated?
- What does it cost, socially or professionally, for an employee on this crew to slow down for a safety concern during a deadline?
- Where in our workflow does production pressure most reliably compress the time available for hazard assessment?
- If I watched a video of my own behavior during the last rushed shift, what would I see my behavior teaching the crew?

Common Field Traps

- Believing that stating 'safety is the priority' is sufficient, while behavior, attention, and consequences consistently signal the opposite.
- Allowing documentation to substitute for verification — when the paperwork is done but the field check is assumed, the paper becomes a liability, not a safeguard.
- Treating pressure-driven shortcuts as individual initiative rather than as a system response to organizational signals.
- Assuming that after a slow period, the crew will automatically re-establish full safety verification — pressure habits persist after the immediate pressure has passed.

- Failing to distinguish between appropriate pace adjustment and unsafe compression of critical verification steps.

Prevention Practices

- Audit your own implicit signals quarterly: what you check on, what gets your reaction, what waits — and compare that to what your stated priorities are.
- Before any high-tempo period, identify the three safety steps most vulnerable to pressure and establish explicit protection for each one.
- Create a visible and genuine response when a crew member slows down for a safety concern during a deadline — your reaction in that moment teaches more than any training.
- After any period of elevated production pressure, conduct a brief review of what safety practices were compressed and what they revealed about the system.
- Separate schedule review from safety review in regular meetings — running them together teaches the workforce that they are competing priorities.

Connection to the 5 How's

The 5 How's provide a structured pressure buffer. When 'How should this task be performed?' and 'How can this fail?' are part of the standing pre-task routine, they resist compression under schedule pressure better than informal planning does. A written question sequence is harder to skip than a mental habit.

Supervisor Toolbox Talk Prompt

Ask your crew: 'When we're behind schedule, what's the first thing that gets shorter — the work or the planning? And what does that tell us about where our real risk is?' This question opens an honest conversation about pressure that most crews are waiting to have.

Chapter Summary

- Pressure changes behavior not by overriding knowledge but by shifting the relative weight of competing priorities — making speed feel more urgent than verification.
- Leaders send dual signals: explicit signals (policies, statements) and implicit signals (behavior, attention, reactions) — when these conflict, implicit signals consistently determine crew behavior.
- The most effective counter to production pressure is the visible, unhurried pause — a leader who stops work without apology teaches the crew that pausing is genuinely acceptable.
- Pressure habits persist after the immediate pressure has passed — recovering safety discipline after a high-tempo period requires deliberate, structured re-establishment.

Leader Action Checklist

[ ] Review what you checked on most often in the last week and compare that list to your stated safety priorities.

[ ] Identify the three safety steps in your operation most vulnerable to schedule pressure and put specific protections in place for each.

[ ] Practice a visible, unhurried safety pause this week — stop a task for verification without apologizing for the time it takes.

[ ] After your next high-tempo period, conduct a five-minute review of what safety practices were compressed and what they revealed.

Chapter 5

FEAR, SILENCE, AND HIDDEN EXPOSURE

Leadership Issue

Exposure that no one talks about is more dangerous than exposure that is visible. When workers know about a hazard but do not report it, do not ask questions about it, and do not raise concerns about the plan, the hazard continues to develop without any organizational response. The silence itself becomes a risk factor. Understanding why employees stop communicating about safety — and what it takes to rebuild that communication — is one of the most important capabilities a safety leader can develop.

The Psychology Behind the Risk

Amy Edmondson's research on psychological safety (1999) established that teams perform better when members feel safe to speak up, ask questions, and admit mistakes without fear of punishment or humiliation. Her research showed that team psychological safety is not about comfort or the absence of conflict — it is about the belief that interpersonal risks are worth taking. In safety-critical environments, this means believing that raising a concern will be received constructively rather than dismissed, mocked, or punished.

When that belief is absent, workers engage in what organizational researchers call 'protective silence' — withholding information not out of indifference, but as a rational response to the social costs of speaking. A worker who raised a concern that was dismissed, a worker who was mocked for slowing down work, a worker who saw a colleague disciplined for reporting a near-miss — these workers learn that silence is the safer personal strategy, even when it is the most dangerous organizational one.

Field Example

Several workers know a task plan is weak, but no one speaks up because the last person who delayed the work was mocked in front of the crew for being overly cautious. The concern is present, the knowledge is present, but the social cost of voicing it exceeds the perceived benefit. The task proceeds with a known flaw. The team knows the flaw exists and completes the task hoping the flaw won't matter today.

Operational Mechanism

The mechanism is learned silence. Each incident of concern dismissal, mockery, or retaliation teaches the workforce a calculation: speaking up costs more than staying quiet. Once that calculation is established, it generalizes beyond the specific incident that produced it. Workers do not re-evaluate the calculation each time — they apply the established pattern. Rebuilding voice after it has been suppressed is significantly harder than maintaining it, because the workforce needs evidence that the pattern has genuinely changed, not just that the language around it has changed.

What Leaders Should Look For

- Toolbox talks and pre-task meetings where questions are limited and agreement is unanimous — not because the plan is flawless, but because questions are not safe.
- Concerns being raised after the task rather than before it — workers who wait until it is over to say they were worried.
- Near-miss reports that describe the hazard but omit the system conditions that contributed to it, suggesting the reporter is self-protecting.
- Workers who consistently say 'everything looks good' regardless of actual conditions.
- A sharp decline in safety observations, near-miss reports, or informal safety conversations following a disciplinary action or a publicly dismissive response to a concern.

Leadership Application

Rebuilding voice after it has been suppressed requires more than declaring that concerns are welcome. Workers who have learned silence do not unlearn it because of a statement — they unlearn it because of repeated behavioral evidence that the pattern has changed. This evidence must be visible, consistent, and include concrete responses to concerns that demonstrate the concern was heard and acted upon.

The most powerful rebuilding behaviors are the smallest ones: thanking someone for a question in a group setting, following up on a concern that was raised informally, and most importantly — making a visible change based on a crew member's observation. When workers see that voicing a concern produces a response and not a cost, the calculation begins to shift.

Leadership Development Focus

Supervisors need to develop the discipline of separating their internal reaction to a concern from their visible response to it. A supervisor who internally disagrees with a worker's concern but visibly engages with it respectfully before making a decision sends a very different message than one whose face or tone communicates dismissal before the words do.

This requires emotional regulation and active listening skills that are not typically taught in safety training. Supervisors should practice the specific behaviors: making eye contact, not interrupting, asking a follow-up question, and thanking the person before moving on. These behaviors are learnable and measurable.

Practical Field Integration

Create a standing practice of acknowledging every concern raised, even when it cannot be immediately acted upon. Acknowledgment has three parts: confirming you heard it, explaining what you will do with it, and following up. The follow-up is the most critical — it is the behavior that determines whether workers conclude that raising concerns is worth the effort.

Track the ratio of concerns raised to concerns resolved. If concerns are being raised but not resolved, workers will eventually stop raising them. The resolution process is more important to voice maintenance than the invitation to speak.

Leadership Questions

- What has happened in this work environment that taught workers the social cost of raising a safety concern?
- What is the most recent concern a worker raised, and what response did it receive — and did the worker see that response?
- Are toolbox talks producing genuine questions or social compliance — and how do I tell the difference?
- What would it take for a worker on this crew to tell me that today's plan is not ready to execute?
- Have I followed up visibly on the last three concerns that were raised — and would the workers who raised them say that they were heard?

Common Field Traps

- Interpreting a quiet, agreeable crew as a safe crew — silence can indicate psychological safety or its complete absence, and the two look identical from the outside.
- Treating concern dismissal as efficient task management — dismissing concerns quickly sends a message that will reduce future reporting.
- Responding to near-miss reports with immediate discipline, which teaches workers that reporting produces punishment rather than learning.
- Assuming that an open-door policy is sufficient — workers who do not believe their concerns will be received well will not use an open door.
- Relying on anonymous reporting systems as a substitute for the daily behavioral signals that either build or suppress voice.

Prevention Practices

- Establish a personal practice: respond to every safety concern raised in a group setting by thanking the person first, regardless of the merit of the concern.
- Track near-miss and concern reporting rates — declining rates after a disciplinary action or dismissive response are a signal requiring immediate attention.
- Build a standing follow-up expectation: every concern raised gets a response within 48 hours, even if that response is only 'I looked into it and here is what I found.'
- Periodically ask a trusted crew member to give you honest feedback on how safe it feels to raise a concern with you — and take the answer seriously.
- Create visible, public responses to crew observations — not necessarily large ones, but ones the crew can see were connected to something a worker said.

Connection to the 5 How's

'How can this task fail?' and 'How will failure be prevented?' only produce useful answers when the crew feels safe to share what they actually know. In an environment where voice has been suppressed, these questions will produce socially acceptable answers rather than honest operational intelligence. Building psychological safety is the prerequisite for the 5 How's to work as intended.

Supervisor Toolbox Talk Prompt

Ask your crew: 'If someone in this group noticed something wrong with today's plan, what would it take for them to say so? And what would get in the way?' Let the answers come. What they describe about the barriers to speaking up tells you exactly what you need to fix.

Chapter Summary

- Workers who know about a hazard but choose not to report it represent one of the most dangerous conditions in any operation — the hazard continues developing without organizational awareness.

- Silence is learned through specific behavioral events: concerns dismissed, reporters mocked, near-misses punished — workers calculate that silence is the safer personal strategy.
- Rebuilding voice after it has been suppressed requires visible, consistent behavioral evidence that the pattern has changed — not just new language or policies.
- The most powerful voice-building behaviors are the smallest: thanking concerns, following up visibly, and making changes that crews can connect to what someone said.

Leader Action Checklist

[ ] Identify the last time a concern was raised in your work area and verify that the person who raised it received a visible, documented response.

[ ] Check your near-miss and observation reporting trend over the last 90 days — a declining trend requires investigation of what suppressed it.

[ ] Practice the three follow-up behaviors this week: acknowledge, explain next steps, follow up with the person.

[ ] Ask one trusted crew member privately how safe it feels to raise a concern during a toolbox talk — and listen to the answer.

Chapter 6

FATIGUE AND THE DECLINE OF AWARENESS

Leadership Issue

Fatigue is not primarily a physical problem. It is a cognitive problem. A fatigued worker may look capable — moving normally, completing tasks, communicating coherently — while operating with significantly degraded judgment, attention, and reaction time. The danger of cognitive fatigue is that the person experiencing it is often the last one to recognize it. Workers who are fatigued frequently underestimate their own impairment, and leaders who have not been trained to recognize fatigue indicators will miss it entirely.

The Psychology Behind the Risk

Research on sleep deprivation and cognitive performance consistently shows that 18–20 hours of wakefulness produces impairment equivalent to a blood alcohol level of approximately 0.10% (Williamson & Feyer, 2000). Unlike alcohol intoxication, however, cognitive fatigue does not produce visible behavioral signals that most observers recognize. A fatigued worker does not slur their words or stumble — they make quiet errors in judgment, miss weak signals, and apply shorter, less rigorous thinking to decisions that require more.

Fatigue also degrades metacognition — the ability to evaluate one's own mental state. This is what makes it particularly dangerous in operational environments: the worker who most needs to slow down, verify, and ask for help is the least likely to recognize that need. Leaders cannot rely on workers to self-report fatigue accurately; they need behavioral indicators and structural protections.

Field Example

Near the end of an overtime shift, a crew wants to finish one final task. Communication becomes short, verification drops, and the desire to be done becomes stronger than the discipline to pause. Confirmation bias sets in — the crew looks for evidence that the task is going well rather than evidence that it is not. Each step feels fine. The cumulative effect of that compressed awareness across the final two hours of the shift is significant.

Operational Mechanism

Cognitive fatigue operates through the progressive degradation of executive function — the mental processes that govern planning, verification, inhibition of impulse, and sustained attention. As fatigue increases, these functions become less reliable while routine procedural responses remain relatively intact. This creates a misleading picture: the worker can still complete routine steps fluently, but their ability to notice when conditions have changed, when the routine does not fit, or when additional verification is needed has declined significantly.

What Leaders Should Look For

- Communication becoming shorter, more abbreviated, or more assumption-based as the shift progresses.
- Verification steps being completed increasingly quickly or by a single person rather than checked by a second person.
- Workers who, when asked a question, take longer to answer or give answers that are less specific than earlier in the shift.
- Reduced responsiveness to new information — workers who are checked out mentally continue executing a plan even when conditions around them have changed.
- An increase in minor errors, restarts, or equipment-handling issues in the final third of a shift or the third consecutive day of overtime.

Leadership Application

Leaders have two tools against fatigue: structural controls and behavioral observation. Structural controls — schedule limits, mandatory rest periods, rotation planning — are the most reliable because they operate before fatigue develops rather than trying to manage it after it has. Behavioral observation — recognizing the indicators in the field — is the backup system for when structural controls are insufficient or have been compromised.

The cultural component is equally important. Crews who normalize fatigue — who treat pushing through exhaustion as professionalism or toughness — are in a more dangerous position than crews who openly discuss fatigue as a risk factor. Leaders who acknowledge fatigue openly, who model the decision to rotate a crew member or end a task, and who do not equate endurance with competence are building a healthier safety culture.

Leadership Development Focus

Supervisors need to develop the ability to assess cognitive readiness, not just physical capability. The question is not 'can this person physically do the job?' but 'is this person's current cognitive state appropriate for the risk level of this task?' Developing this assessment skill requires knowing what cognitive fatigue looks like in specific individuals — some people become quiet, some become irritable, some become overconfident. The baseline matters.

Practical Field Integration

Build fatigue indicators into your pre-task observation checklist. Before high-risk or non-routine work, spend two minutes observing the crew's communication quality, response speed, and engagement level. Compare what you observe to what you would expect from a well-rested crew at the start of a shift. If there is a significant gap, that is information to act on.

Also build end-of-shift reviews into your routine that specifically examine whether the final hours of the shift produced any indicators of degraded awareness — near misses, communication failures, or error recovery events that the crew handled but that would not have occurred at the start of the shift.

Leadership Questions

- At what point in the shift or workweek does the quality of pre-task planning, verification, and communication start to decline in this crew?
- What behavioral signals tell me that a specific worker's cognitive readiness is not adequate for the risk level of the current task?
- Have I built the structural protections — rotation, task sequencing, mandatory pause points — that reduce reliance on individuals to self-report fatigue?
- What does the culture around fatigue on this crew look like — is it discussed as a risk factor or normalized as a mark of professionalism?
- In the last month, what incidents, near-misses, or quality issues occurred in the final hours of a shift or at the end of a multi-day push?

Common Field Traps

- Equating physical endurance with cognitive readiness — a worker who is physically capable of continuing may have significantly degraded judgment.
- Relying on workers to self-report fatigue, when research consistently shows that fatigued individuals underestimate their own impairment.
- Treating the final task of a shift as lower-risk because it is almost done — in many cases, it carries higher risk because crew cognitive reserves are lowest.
- Normalizing overtime as a routine operational response rather than a condition that requires specific risk management.
- Responding to fatigue-related incidents with individual accountability rather than structural change — if the structure creates the fatigue, punishing the individual does not prevent the next incident.

Prevention Practices

- Identify your highest-risk tasks and build a standing rule that they are not performed in the final two hours of an extended shift or the third consecutive overtime day.
- Build end-of-shift communication quality checks into your observation routine — comparison to start-of-shift behavior identifies fatigue-related decline.
- Normalize the fatigue conversation: make it standard practice in pre-task talks to ask how people feel and to treat the answer seriously.
- Create rotation schedules for high-concentration tasks that ensure cognitive freshness rather than maximizing hours on task.
- Review your overtime authorization process to determine whether schedule pressure is systematically overriding fatigue management.

Connection to the 5 How's

Fatigue degrades every element of the 5 How's. A tired crew asking 'how can this task fail?' produces shallower answers. 'How will controls be verified?' is abbreviated or skipped. The 5 How's require cognitive resources that fatigue consumes. This means fatigue management is not separate from operational planning — it is a precondition for planning quality.

Supervisor Toolbox Talk Prompt

Try this at the start of a late-shift or overtime task: 'I want to check in honestly before we start. Rate your mental sharpness right now from 1 to 10. If anyone is below a 7, I want to know — because what we're about to do needs more than 60% of our thinking.' Watch what happens to the conversation.

Chapter Summary

- Cognitive fatigue degrades judgment, attention, and error-detection long before physical capability declines — the worker experiencing it is often the last to recognize it.

- Structural controls — schedule limits, rotation planning, mandatory rest — are more reliable than behavioral observation because they operate before fatigue develops.
- Workers who normalize fatigue as a mark of professionalism are in a more dangerous position than those who treat it as a risk factor that requires management.
- The final hours of an extended shift or overtime period are not lower-risk simply because the work is almost done — they are often higher-risk because cognitive reserves are lowest.

Leader Action Checklist

[ ] Identify the highest-risk tasks in your operation and verify they are not routinely scheduled for the final hours of extended shifts.

[ ] Build a cognitive readiness check into your pre-task observation for any task following more than 10 hours of work or three consecutive overtime days.

[ ] Review the last month's near-misses and incidents and check whether any occurred in the final third of a shift or during a sustained overtime period.

[ ] Have one honest conversation with your crew this week about fatigue as a risk factor — not as a sign of weakness but as a cognitive condition that requires management.

Chapter 7

TASK FIXATION AND OPERATIONAL BLINDNESS

Leadership Issue

Attention is finite. When a worker becomes deeply focused on a specific task, their ability to perceive information outside that narrow focus decreases significantly. In operational environments, this narrowing of attention — sometimes called tunneling — is one of the most common contributors to incidents involving otherwise experienced workers. The person involved was not inattentive. They were intensely attentive to the wrong thing at the wrong time.

The Psychology Behind the Risk

The psychological phenomenon of inattentional blindness, demonstrated by Simons and Chabris (1999), shows that people engaged in a focused task reliably fail to notice conspicuous, unexpected events occurring in their direct field of vision. The brain is not passively recording everything in the environment — it is actively constructing a representation based on what it has been directed to attend to. When that direction is narrow, the representation is narrow.

In safety-critical work, task fixation is most dangerous during troubleshooting, diagnosis, and problem-solving — the moments when cognitive engagement is highest. These are also the moments when conditions around the worker are most likely to be changing, when coworker positioning matters most, and when energy state and equipment configuration must be continuously monitored. The depth of focus that makes a skilled technician effective at diagnosis is the same cognitive state that produces blindness to adjacent hazards.

Field Example

During troubleshooting, a technician focuses so intensely on restoring equipment that changing energy state, coworker position, and nearby movement fade from awareness. The technician is not negligent — they are doing exactly what their training and experience have prepared them to do: diagnose and solve the problem. The adjacent hazards are visible but not perceived, because perception has been entirely allocated to the task at hand.

Operational Mechanism

Task fixation is amplified by three conditions that frequently co-occur in operational environments: time pressure, problem novelty, and high personal investment in solving the problem. A technician troubleshooting an unfamiliar failure under schedule pressure, with the crew waiting and the supervisor watching, is in exactly the conditions that produce maximum fixation and minimum peripheral awareness. Leaders who add pressure to these situations compound the risk.

What Leaders Should Look For

- Workers who do not acknowledge or respond to verbal communication during complex task execution — not because they are ignoring it, but because they genuinely did not perceive it.
- Crew members whose physical positioning during focused work does not reflect awareness of their surroundings — backs to hazards, tools placed without clearing adjacent work.
- Tasks where one person becomes the designated problem-solver while others disengage — this creates both fixation in the problem-solver and diffusion of situational awareness in the group.
- Troubleshooting situations where no one is designated to maintain environmental awareness while the technical work is being done.

- Post-task accounts from workers who report being surprised by conditions that were clearly visible during the task — 'I didn't even notice that was there.'

Leadership Application

The operational response to task fixation is the designated lookout or spotter role: assigning one person in a focused work situation to maintain environmental awareness while the technical work is performed. This is not a new concept — it appears in confined space, crane, and high-voltage work procedures. But it is under-applied in the broader range of operational situations where fixation actually occurs, including equipment troubleshooting, complex repair work, and multi-stage maintenance tasks.

Leaders should also build pause-and-scan behaviors into high-risk task execution — deliberate moments where the worker stops, steps back mentally, and re-surveys the environment before continuing. These moments are most useful at task transition points, at any point where conditions change, and at any point where the worker's focus has been narrowed for more than a few minutes.

Leadership Development Focus

Supervisors need to develop the ability to recognize when a worker is in a fixation state and to intervene constructively. The challenge is that interrupting a focused worker at the wrong moment can itself create a hazard — disrupting a critical procedure, causing a loss of task state, or triggering an error of omission. The skill is interrupting with a question that resets awareness without disrupting task execution: 'Take a second — what are you seeing around you right now?' rather than 'Watch out!'

Practical Field Integration

For tasks that historically produce fixation-related incidents — troubleshooting, complex repair, high-focus diagnostic work — build a standing structural protection: one person on the task is designated to maintain environmental awareness and is not assigned to the technical problem. This role rotates so everyone on the crew develops both the technical focus skill and the environmental awareness skill.

Also build post-task fixation reviews into your learning process. When a worker reports not noticing a condition that was clearly present, treat that as operational intelligence about where fixation structures are needed, not as an individual failure.

Leadership Questions

- Which tasks in our operation are most likely to produce deep cognitive fixation — and what structural protections exist for those tasks?
- During our last complex troubleshooting event, who was responsible for maintaining environmental awareness while the technical work was being done?
- What conditions — pressure, novelty, personal investment — are most likely to produce maximum fixation on this crew?
- How do I interrupt a worker who is in a fixation state without disrupting a critical procedure or creating a secondary error?
- What post-task accounts have I heard that included surprised workers — workers who did not notice something that was present — and what do those accounts reveal?

Common Field Traps

- Praising intense focus and concentration without recognizing that these states reduce peripheral awareness — 'he's so focused' can describe both competence and a risk state.
- Assuming that experienced workers automatically maintain situational awareness during complex tasks — fixation increases with task complexity regardless of experience level.
- Adding verbal pressure to a worker in a fixation state — asking urgency questions or creating interruptions that fragment attention without rebuilding it.
- Failing to designate environmental awareness responsibilities during high-focus work, leaving that function to whoever has mental bandwidth left over.

- Treating fixation-related incidents as inattention or distraction, which leads to reminders and warnings rather than structural changes to how focused work is organized.

Prevention Practices

- For troubleshooting, diagnostic, and complex repair tasks, establish a standing role assignment: one person on task execution, one person on environmental monitoring.
- Build mandatory pause-and-scan points into your procedure for tasks that require sustained high-focus over extended periods.
- Reduce fixation-amplifying conditions where possible: provide realistic timelines for complex troubleshooting, reduce audience pressure during diagnostic work, and allow workers to stop and think without social cost.
- Develop a crew-level signal — verbal or physical — that any worker can use to call a pause-and-scan without disrupting the technical task.
- Include fixation awareness in new supervisor training: what does it look like, how do you interrupt it constructively, and what structural protections should be built into high-focus task planning.

Connection to the 5 How's

The 5 How's address fixation risk directly through 'How can this task fail?' When fixation is explicitly named as a failure mode in pre-task planning — 'one failure mode is that our technician becomes so focused on the repair that they stop monitoring energy state' — the crew has a shared language for the risk and a prompt for the countermeasure.

Supervisor Toolbox Talk Prompt

Ask your crew: 'Think about the last time you were deeply focused on solving a problem. What was happening around you that you weren't aware of? What would you have missed if something had gone wrong nearby?' This question makes the experience of fixation visible and starts the conversation about structural protections.

Chapter Summary

- Task fixation is not inattention — it is intense attention directed narrowly, leaving adjacent hazards and environmental changes outside of conscious perception.
- Fixation is amplified by time pressure, task novelty, and personal investment in solving the problem — the exact conditions that characterize complex troubleshooting and emergency response.
- The most reliable structural protection is role designation: one person focused on the technical task, one person responsible for environmental awareness.
- Post-task accounts of surprise — workers who did not notice conditions that were present — are fixation intelligence that should inform structural changes, not individual feedback.

Leader Action Checklist

[ ] Identify the three tasks in your operation most likely to produce cognitive fixation and evaluate what environmental monitoring role exists for each.

[ ] Build a pause-and-scan expectation into your next complex troubleshooting or high-focus task.

[ ] Practice the constructive fixation interruption question with your crew this week: 'Take a second — what are you seeing around you right now?'

[ ] Review recent near-misses for any accounts of worker surprise at conditions they did not notice — these indicate where fixation structures are needed.

PART II — COMMUNICATION AND LEADERSHIP PSYCHOLOGY

Safety depends on communication as much as it depends on controls. Part II examines the psychological dynamics of communication in operational environments — why stress disrupts it, why employees stop engaging in it, and how leadership behavior either builds or destroys the conditions under which honest, accurate communication is possible.

Chapter 8

STRESS, EMOTION, AND COMMUNICATION BREAKDOWN

Leadership Issue

Stress does not just make people feel bad — it changes how they communicate. Under stress, the human brain shifts from complex, nuanced processing to faster, more defensive patterns. Communication becomes shorter, less precise, and less receptive to input that conflicts with a current course of action. In safety-critical environments where clear, accurate communication is a core control, stress-induced communication breakdown is a direct risk factor — not a personnel problem or a soft-skills issue.

The Psychology Behind the Risk

The neurological basis of stress-induced communication change is well-established. The amygdala's threat response reduces prefrontal cortex activity — the part of the brain responsible for complex reasoning, empathy, and regulated response. Under acute stress, people become more reactive, less accurate in processing social cues, and more likely to communicate in ways that escalate tension rather than reduce it (LeDoux, 1996). In work environments, this manifests as shorter instructions, less verification, increased use of assumption-based communication, and reduced willingness to ask clarifying questions.

Emotional contagion compounds the effect. When one member of a team is visibly stressed, anxious, or frustrated, those emotions transfer to other team members through tone, body language, and response patterns. A supervisor who communicates urgency through compressed, terse instructions does not just shorten their own communication — they trigger a compressed, terse communication pattern across the whole crew.

Field Example

A disagreement during a rushed lift plan becomes emotional. The technical issue is manageable, but the tone causes people to stop asking clarifying questions. One person withdraws from the conversation to avoid conflict. Another continues asserting without listening. The plan proceeds with unresolved ambiguity that everyone felt but no one voiced after the emotional temperature rose.

Operational Mechanism

The mechanism is dual: internal regulation failure and social contagion. When a leader's emotional state changes, the crew's communication pattern mirrors it — often before anyone has explicitly acknowledged the stress. A supervisor who is visibly frustrated with a schedule delay may not say anything unsafe, but the crew reads the frustration and adjusts their communication accordingly: shorter questions, fewer pauses, less willingness to raise concerns that might add to the frustration. The communication environment changes without any explicit instruction.

What Leaders Should Look For

- Communication exchanges that have shortened significantly from the beginning to the middle of a task — fewer words, more assumptions, less verification.
- Crew members who stop asking questions after a tone change, not because their questions were answered but because the environment became unwelcoming.

- Leaders whose communication style compresses noticeably under deadline pressure — more directive, less receptive, shorter planning discussions.
- Physical signals of stress spreading through a crew: tightened posture, reduced eye contact, faster movements without corresponding purpose.
- Plans that proceed after visible disagreement without explicit resolution — situations where the disagreement was abandoned rather than resolved.

Leadership Application

The leader's first responsibility under stress is self-regulation — managing their own emotional state before it contaminates the crew's communication environment. This is not about suppressing emotion or pretending stress does not exist. It is about deliberately pausing before communicating under stress, choosing tone consciously, and modeling the behavior that keeps the team's communication channel open.

A practical technique is the pre-communication pause: before issuing any instruction under high-stress conditions, take two seconds, regulate tone, and ask whether the instruction is as clear as it needs to be. Two seconds is almost imperceptibly brief to the crew but can change the quality of what is communicated significantly.

Leadership Development Focus

Supervisors need development in stress communication specifically — not just general communication skills, but communication under the actual conditions they experience at work: behind schedule, under observation, managing competing demands, dealing with disagreements in a time-compressed environment. Role-play and scenario practice that simulate those conditions are more effective than classroom instruction that assumes optimal communication conditions.

Practical Field Integration

Build stress-communication checkpoints into your high-tension operational situations. Before a critical lift, before a difficult conversation, before a task plan that involves disagreement — pause the group and establish communication ground rules explicitly: 'We need to hear from everyone before we proceed. Questions don't delay us; proceeding with unresolved questions does.'

After high-stress events, debrief the communication quality specifically: what questions were not asked, what concerns were not voiced, and what the communication breakdown revealed about the plan.

Leadership Questions

- What does my own communication look like under the specific stressors I experience at work, and what does the crew hear differently than what I intend?
- After the last high-stress operational event, what concerns existed in the crew that were not voiced because of the emotional environment?
- What is the signal in my team's communication that tells me emotional contagion is occurring — that stress is spreading through the group?
- Which individuals on my crew are most likely to withdraw from communication under stress, and what do I miss when they disengage?
- How would I run this pre-task discussion differently if I were not under schedule pressure — and what does the difference tell me about where risk is developing?

Common Field Traps

- Treating stress-induced communication breakdown as a personality conflict rather than a cognitive response to conditions — this leads to people management rather than system improvement.

- Interpreting a crew that communicates well under normal conditions as a crew that communicates well under stress — the two are not the same capability.
- Using terse, directive communication under pressure and calling it efficiency — abbreviated communication under stress creates ambiguity that has to be resolved during task execution, not before it.
- Failing to address a communication breakdown until it produces an incident — the breakdown itself is the event that requires a response.
- Assuming that stress communication is primarily an individual issue — emotional contagion means it is always a system issue requiring system-level responses.

Prevention Practices

- Develop and practice a personal stress-communication pause: before issuing any instruction under high-stress conditions, deliberately regulate tone and verify clarity.
- Build pre-task communication ground rules into your highest-tension operational situations — name the expectation explicitly: 'We hear everyone before we proceed.'
- After any event involving elevated stress, debrief the communication quality as a separate item: what was not asked, what was not said, and what that reveals.
- Identify the individuals on your crew who disengage from communication under stress and build specific practices to include their input before those situations develop.
- Practice recognizing your own emotional contagion signal — the moment when your stress state begins visibly affecting the crew — and develop a response for that moment.

Connection to the 5 How's

Communication quality determines the quality of 5 How's responses. If the pre-task environment is stressed and emotionally compressed, the crew's answers to 'how can this task fail?' will be shorter, less complete, and less honest. The 5 How's framework is only as strong as the communication environment in which it is applied.

Supervisor Toolbox Talk Prompt

Ask your crew: 'On a day when we're behind and pressure is high, what changes about how we talk to each other — and what safety-critical information are we most likely to miss because of that change?' This conversation builds collective awareness of stress communication patterns before the next high-pressure situation occurs.

Chapter Summary

- Stress changes communication neurologically — the brain shifts to faster, more defensive patterns that produce shorter instructions, fewer questions, and less receptivity to conflicting information.
- Emotional contagion means a leader's stress state transfers to the crew's communication pattern, often before anyone has acknowledged the stress explicitly.
- Self-regulation before communication — not suppression of emotion, but deliberate management of tone and clarity under stress — is the leader's first responsibility.
- Post-event communication debriefs that examine what was not said are as important as task debriefs that examine what went wrong.

Leader Action Checklist

[ ] Practice the pre-communication pause this week during at least one high-pressure situation — two seconds of deliberate tone regulation before issuing an instruction.

[ ] After your next high-stress operational event, debrief the communication quality specifically: what questions were not asked and what concerns were not voiced?

[ ] Identify one crew member who disengages from communication under stress and build one practice to include their input before the next high-pressure situation.

[ ] Observe your own communication during a period of schedule pressure and note the difference between how you communicate under pressure and under normal conditions.

Chapter 9

WHY EMPLOYEES STOP SPEAKING UP

Leadership Issue

Every safety system that relies on workers reporting hazards, near-misses, and concerns depends on a single precondition: workers who believe that speaking up is worth it. When that belief erodes, reporting declines, concerns remain hidden, and the organization loses its earliest and most valuable source of safety intelligence. The loss is often gradual and invisible — not a single event but a slow withdrawal of employee voice over weeks or months.

The Psychology Behind the Risk

Seligman's research on learned helplessness (1972) provides a direct psychological model for reporting fatigue: when individuals repeatedly take action without producing a meaningful outcome, they learn to stop taking that action. Applied to safety reporting, a worker who raises concerns that are dismissed, ignored, or produce no visible response learns that reporting is effortful without benefit. The calculation shifts, and the reporting stops.

Morrison and Milliken's (2000) research on organizational silence identified two primary drivers of employee voice suppression: the belief that speaking up is futile (nothing will change), and the belief that speaking up is risky (personal costs will follow). Both must be addressed for reporting culture to function. Addressing only one is insufficient — a worker who believes it is safe to report but futile to do so will eventually stop just as completely as one who fears punishment.

Field Example

A worker who reported repeated barricade issues twice and saw no correction eventually stops reporting them. The hazard did not disappear; the reporting did. The worker did not become careless

— they became realistic. They concluded, based on evidence, that the effort of reporting produced no protective benefit and therefore was not worth repeating. That conclusion is rational within their experience, and only a change in organizational response will change it.

Operational Mechanism

Voice erosion operates through the accumulation of reporting experiences. Each unacknowledged report, each dismissed concern, each near-miss that produced punishment rather than learning adds to a private calculation about the value of reporting. The calculation is individual — different workers have different thresholds — but the pattern is systemic. When multiple workers independently arrive at the same conclusion about the value of reporting, the organization has created a reporting culture problem through its response patterns.

What Leaders Should Look For

- A declining trend in near-miss reports, observation reports, or informal safety concerns following a period of no visible responses to previous reports.
- Workers who describe hazards or concerns informally but have not logged them through formal reporting channels.
- Toolbox talk participation declining over time — workers who no longer ask questions or raise issues they raised readily six months earlier.
- Workers who preface concerns with apologies or qualifications — 'I'm probably wrong, but...' — indicating that speaking up carries a social cost they are trying to preemptively manage.
- Supervisors who are surprised by hazards their crew knew about but had stopped reporting.

Leadership Application

The two drivers of voice suppression require two distinct responses. For futility — the belief that nothing will change — the response is visible action connected to reports: when a worker reports something, something happens, and the worker sees that it happened. The connection between report and response must be explicit and timely. 'You mentioned the barricade two weeks ago — we completed the fix yesterday. Thank you' is more powerful than any policy statement about reporting culture.

For risk — the belief that speaking up carries personal cost — the response is behavioral: demonstrating through specific, visible leadership actions that safety concerns are received with respect and gratitude rather than with dismissal or retaliation. This takes longer to rebuild than to establish, because workers who have been burned require more evidence than workers whose trust has not yet been tested.

Leadership Development Focus

Supervisors need to develop the habit of closing the loop — connecting their response to a concern back to the person who raised it. This is one of the most consistently neglected behaviors in safety leadership because it requires tracking, follow-through, and time. But it is also one of the most powerful voice-maintenance behaviors available. A supervisor who closes the loop consistently, even on minor concerns, builds a reporting culture without needing to announce it.

Practical Field Integration

Implement a visible reporting response board or communication mechanism — not just a tracking system for compliance purposes, but a visible display of concerns raised and actions taken that the crew can see. The purpose is to demonstrate the connection between reporting and response at a level of visibility that changes the crew's calculation about whether reporting is worth the effort.

Also audit your reporting trend monthly. A flat or declining trend is a leading indicator that something has changed in the cost-benefit calculation workers are making. Do not wait for the trend to become severe before investigating its cause.

Leadership Questions

- What was the last concern my crew raised, what response did it receive, and did the worker who raised it see that response?
- Looking at my reporting trend over the last six months, when did it change, and what happened around that time?
- Are there workers on my crew who used to report actively and no longer do — and what changed in their experience?
- What does a worker on this crew believe will happen after they submit a safety report — and how accurate is that belief?
- What concerns has my crew raised informally that were never formally logged — and what does that gap tell me about the reporting culture?

Common Field Traps

- Measuring reporting culture by report volume without examining whether the response rate and quality have been adequate — high report volume can mask poor response, and poor response eventually reduces volume.
- Treating a quiet reporting period as evidence of good conditions rather than investigating whether voice suppression has occurred.
- Responding to a near-miss with visible punishment and then being surprised that subsequent near-miss reporting declines.
- Assuming that anonymous reporting systems resolve the voice suppression problem — anonymity removes the social cost of reporting but does not address the futility calculation.
- Conflating compliance-driven reporting (required forms) with voluntary safety intelligence (concerns workers choose to share) — the two are not the same and require different management.

Prevention Practices

- Implement a standing close-the-loop practice: every reported concern receives a response connected to the person who reported it, within 48 hours.

- Track your reporting trend monthly and investigate the cause of any declining pattern before it becomes severe.
- Create visible evidence that reporting produces response: a communication mechanism that shows concerns raised and actions taken.
- Conduct periodic one-on-one conversations with crew members about whether they have concerns they have not formally reported — and ask why.
- Review the response your team received after the last three near-miss or hazard reports and evaluate whether those responses reinforced or discouraged future reporting.

Connection to the 5 How's

Reporting and near-miss information are the primary inputs for 'How can this task fail?' and 'How will we improve?' If workers have stopped reporting, the 5 How's conversation lacks its most current and field-accurate information. Voice maintenance is not separate from preventive analysis — it is the data collection system that makes preventive analysis possible.

Supervisor Toolbox Talk Prompt

Ask your crew: 'Think about the last concern or near-miss you decided not to report. What made you decide not to report it? I'm asking because understanding what gets in the way of reporting is as important as understanding the hazard itself.' Create space for honest answers — and take the answers seriously.

Chapter Summary

- Voice erosion is gradual and based on accumulated experience — workers stop reporting when their reports consistently produce no visible response or when reporting has historically carried personal cost.
- Two distinct drivers of silence require two distinct responses: for futility (nothing changes), visible action connected to reports; for risk (speaking up costs me), behavioral demonstration that concerns are received with respect.

- Closing the loop — connecting the organizational response back to the person who reported — is one of the most powerful and most neglected voice-maintenance behaviors in safety leadership.
- A declining reporting trend is a leading indicator of a cultural problem that requires investigation of the cause, not simply encouragement to report more.

Leader Action Checklist

[ ] Review your last three near-miss or hazard reports and verify that each reporter received an explicit response connected back to them.

[ ] Check your reporting trend over the past six months and identify any declining periods — investigate what changed around those periods.

[ ] Have one honest conversation this week with a crew member about whether they have concerns they have not formally reported.

[ ] Create or update a visible reporting response mechanism that the crew can see — showing what was reported and what was done.

Chapter 10

GROUP BEHAVIOR AND CREW PSYCHOLOGY

Leadership Issue

Individual behavior and group behavior follow different rules. A worker who would pause and ask a question alone may not ask that question in a group. A worker who privately disagrees with a plan may not voice that disagreement in a crew meeting. A worker who has a private concern about a condition may interpret the group's apparent acceptance of that condition as evidence that their concern is wrong. Understanding how group dynamics suppress individual safety behavior is essential for any leader who runs work through crews, teams, or shifts.

The Psychology Behind the Risk

Asch's conformity research (1951) demonstrated that individuals will publicly agree with a clearly incorrect group answer rather than stand out as different. In safety contexts, this means workers will accept plans they privately believe are inadequate rather than be the person who delays the work or questions the supervisor. The pressure to conform is not primarily about fear of punishment — it operates through a more subtle social mechanism: the desire to be seen as competent, aligned, and not difficult.

Latané and Darley's research on the bystander effect (1970) showed that diffusion of responsibility increases as group size grows: each individual in a group feels less personal responsibility for a problem because they assume others are more appropriately positioned to respond. Applied to safety, this means that in a larger crew, each individual is less likely to be the one who raises a concern — they assume someone with more authority or more relevant knowledge will do it. In many cases, no one does.

Field Example

A new employee notices a shortcut that does not match the procedure they were trained on. They look at the experienced workers and see everyone doing it. Within their first week, they have adopted the same shortcut — not because they were told to, but because the group's behavior communicated that this is how the work is actually done. The group's behavior rewrote the training without a single conversation.

Operational Mechanism

Social proof is the mechanism: in ambiguous situations, people look to the behavior of others as information about what is appropriate. When the crew does not stop for verification, the implicit message is that verification is not needed here. When experienced workers move confidently through a hazard zone, the message is that the hazard is not serious enough to warrant caution. Group behavior teaches faster and more powerfully than any formal training program, because it operates in real time, in the real work environment, through people the worker trusts.

What Leaders Should Look For

- New employees who adopt crew-specific shortcuts within the first few weeks — faster than any formal acclimation would explain.
- Unanimous agreement in pre-task meetings among workers who have different levels of experience with the task — true consensus is rare and should be verified.
- Situations where no one speaks up about a visible problem because everyone is waiting for someone else to address it.
- Experienced workers whose behavior would be flagged as unsafe if done by a new employee but is accepted without comment because of their tenure.
- Group behavior that is internally inconsistent — the crew follows the rule when a supervisor is present and sets it aside when the supervisor is absent.

Leadership Application

Leaders should deliberately structure pre-task discussions to prevent social conformity from producing false consensus. One effective technique is the sequential question: ask each person in the group individually before inviting general discussion. This captures private opinions before social influence can suppress them. A worker who has a private concern is more likely to voice it when asked directly than when expected to raise it in a group environment.

Leaders should also identify and actively manage the informal authority figures on their crew — the experienced workers whose behavior functions as social proof for everyone else. When these individuals model safe behavior, their influence multiplies the leader's efforts. When they model shortcuts, their influence multiplies the risk.

Leadership Development Focus

Supervisors need to understand that their formal authority is only one source of influence in a crew environment. Informal authority — the credibility and influence held by experienced workers, vocal personalities, and social hubs within the crew — shapes behavior as much or more than formal position. Identifying and understanding the informal authority structure in their crew gives supervisors a more accurate picture of how behavior is actually being shaped.

Practical Field Integration

Build structured individual response moments into your pre-task discussions. Before asking 'does everyone agree with the plan?' establish a practice of asking each person a specific, answerable question: 'What is your biggest concern about this task today?' Individual responses before group discussion produce more accurate information about actual crew knowledge and readiness.

Also use group behavior diagnostics: compare how the crew behaves when you are present to how they behave when you are not. A significant difference is not a supervision problem — it is a culture problem, and it requires a different response than increased monitoring.

Leadership Questions

- Which informal authority figures on this crew are most influencing behavior — and is that influence pointed toward the safety standards or away from them?
- In the last group planning discussion, who did not speak — and what might they have said if asked directly?
- Where does crew behavior change when the supervisor is not present, and what does that difference reveal about the culture versus the compliance?
- What behaviors has this crew collectively normalized that an outside observer would identify as inconsistent with our standards?
- When was the last time a new employee was protected from a crew-established shortcut rather than absorbed into it?

Common Field Traps

- Interpreting group silence as consensus — in most crew environments, silence means social conformity, not agreement.
- Managing only formal authority figures while leaving informal authority figures unaddressed — the experienced worker whose behavior is social proof for the crew may have more influence than the supervisor.
- Using group-level accountability for individual behavior, which diffuses responsibility further rather than assigning it clearly.
- Treating new employee adoption of crew shortcuts as a training failure rather than a culture transmission event — the crew is doing the training, and it is working.
- Assuming that a crew with high morale has a safe culture — positive group dynamics and safe group norms are not the same thing.

Prevention Practices

- Implement sequential individual questioning in pre-task discussions before opening to group discussion — private opinions before social influence.
- Identify the informal authority figures on your crew and deliberately engage them in modeling the behaviors you want the group to adopt.
- Conduct periodic comparison observations — how the crew behaves with you present versus without you — and use the difference as a culture diagnostic.
- Protect new employees from early crew-based shortcut adoption by building a specific first-30-days observation and conversation practice.
- Build a standing expectation that consensus in a pre-task discussion requires each person to voice agreement explicitly, not simply to not object.

Connection to the 5 How's

Group dynamics affect the quality of 5 How's discussions directly. When social conformity is operating, 'how can this task fail?' produces the socially acceptable answer rather than the operationally accurate one. Structuring the 5 How's discussion to capture individual responses before group consensus is formed produces more honest and more useful answers.

Supervisor Toolbox Talk Prompt

Try this: before your next pre-task discussion, tell the crew, 'I'm going to ask each of you one question individually before we talk as a group. The question is: what is your one biggest concern about today's task?' Then go around the group. What comes up when people answer individually almost always differs from what comes up in open group discussion.

Chapter Summary

- Individual behavior in groups follows different rules than individual behavior alone — social pressure, diffusion of responsibility, and social proof consistently suppress individual safety behavior in group settings.

- Group behavior functions as informal training for new employees — it overwrites formal training more rapidly and effectively than any official program.
- Informal authority figures — experienced workers whose behavior is social proof for the crew — may have more influence on group behavior than the formal supervisor.
- Pre-task discussions that invite group consensus before capturing individual opinions produce false agreement that conceals genuine concerns.

Leader Action Checklist

[ ] Identify the two or three informal authority figures on your crew and evaluate whether their observable behavior supports or undermines the safety standards.

[ ] Try sequential individual questioning in your next pre-task discussion and compare what you learn to what you learn from open group discussion.

[ ] Observe how the crew behaves in your absence compared to your presence and investigate any significant differences.

[ ] Check whether any new employees in their first 30 days have adopted crew-level shortcuts — and respond to that as a culture transmission event.

Chapter 11

LEADERSHIP TONE AND HUMAN RESPONSE

Leadership Issue

Leadership tone is not a soft skill. It is an operational variable that directly determines how much safety-relevant information reaches the leader and how reliably the workforce follows safety standards when no one is watching. A leader whose tone communicates that safety concerns are welcome and that pausing for verification is respected will receive more safety intelligence from the field than a leader whose tone — regardless of stated policy — communicates impatience, dismissal, or production priority.

The Psychology Behind the Risk

Organizational climate research consistently shows that the psychological climate created by direct supervisors has a stronger influence on employee behavior than organizational policy (Zohar, 2002). Employees form their behavioral response to safety expectations based primarily on what they observe their immediate supervisor doing, rewarding, and tolerating — not on what corporate policy states. This is sometimes called the 'signals and signs' effect: the signals sent by supervisory behavior are more powerful than the formal signs of organizational safety systems.

Psychological safety research (Edmondson, 1999) shows that teams perform better when leaders create an interpersonal environment in which people feel safe to take risks — to ask questions, admit mistakes, and raise concerns. The leader's tone is the primary determinant of whether that environment exists. A leader who regularly communicates frustration with interruptions, dismisses concerns as overcaution, or visibly prioritizes speed over verification is actively destroying the conditions under which safety information travels.

Field Example

A manager says safety matters, but reacts with visible frustration whenever work pauses for reassessment. The words are right. The tone is not. Employees learn — quickly and accurately — that stopping work is technically allowed but emotionally unwelcome. The safer personal strategy is to continue, adapt, and not be the person who triggers the frustration. Safety information stops flowing toward the leader.

Operational Mechanism

The mechanism is emotional calibration: workers continuously calibrate their behavior to match what produces positive responses from the leader. This calibration is largely unconscious and operates through emotional signals — tone of voice, body language, attentional focus, visible emotional reactions — rather than through explicit instruction. A leader's most powerful communication is usually not their words.

What Leaders Should Look For

- Workers who deliver safety concerns with preemptive apologies or who preface observations with 'I'm probably wrong, but...' — indicating that disagreeing with the leader carries a social cost.
- Crews whose questions and concerns cluster during periods when a specific supervisor is not present.
- Post-task conversations where workers mention that they noticed a concern but 'didn't want to slow things down.'
- A pattern where safety concerns raised by certain supervisors' crews are consistently less specific and less actionable than concerns raised by other crews.
- Workers who express relief rather than satisfaction after completing tasks safely — relief indicates they were managing risk they did not feel they could voice.

Leadership Application

Tone change requires behavioral specificity. Generic resolve to 'be more supportive' produces little actual change because it lacks behavioral definition. The specific behaviors that constitute a constructive safety tone include: making eye contact when someone raises a concern, asking a follow-up question before responding, completing the pause before resuming rather than suggesting the concern be 'noted and addressed later,' and expressing visible satisfaction — not just tolerance — when a worker pauses the work for safety.

These behaviors can be practiced and measured. Supervisors who receive feedback on these specific behaviors and practice them under realistic work conditions change their tone in ways that produce measurable increases in safety reporting and concern-raising.

Leadership Development Focus

Tone development requires that supervisors receive accurate feedback on how they actually come across — which is almost always different from how they believe they come across. This requires observation by a trusted coach or peer who can describe specific behavioral signals rather than general impressions. 'You seemed frustrated' is not as useful as 'when the work stopped for the question about the barricade, your body language tightened and you looked at your watch before responding.'

Practical Field Integration

Conduct a periodic tone audit: ask a trusted crew member or colleague to observe you during a representative work period and describe specifically what your tone is communicating — not your words, but your body language, your emotional responses, and your attentional behavior. Use that feedback to identify specific behaviors to change, not general impressions to manage.

Also build a deliberate practice of the 'welcome signal' — a visible, consistent behavioral response when a worker raises a concern that communicates genuine appreciation rather than tolerance.

Leadership Questions

- What does my tone communicate about whether pausing work for safety is genuinely welcome, versus technically permitted but unwelcome?
- What specific behaviors do I use consistently when a worker raises a safety concern — and what message do those behaviors send?
- Which workers on my crew raise concerns most readily, and which rarely do — and what is different about how they experience my response?
- If I asked my crew privately what my tone communicates about what I actually care about, what would they say?
- When was the last time I visibly expressed satisfaction — not just acceptance — when someone stopped work for a safety concern?

Common Field Traps

- Believing that stated policy overrides behavioral signals — workers calibrate to behavior, not to policy statements.
- Conflating 'my door is open' with an open communication tone — physical access and psychological access are different things.
- Treating tone as fixed personality rather than as learnable behavior — tone is composed of specific, observable behaviors that can be changed.
- Measuring tone impact by whether the leader intends to be welcoming rather than whether workers actually experience it as welcoming.
- Responding to declining reporting with more requests for reports rather than examining the tone conditions that are suppressing them.

Prevention Practices

- Identify three specific behaviors that constitute your 'welcome signal' for safety concerns — and practice them deliberately.

- Request a behavioral tone observation from a peer or trusted team member during a representative work period — ask for specific behavioral descriptions, not general impressions.
- Build a deliberate practice of the follow-up question before responding to any safety concern: ask one question before offering your own view.
- Audit the last week's interactions for the ratio of expressed satisfaction to expressed frustration when work paused for safety reasons.
- Create a personal standard: after any worker raises a safety concern, your visible response before any words are spoken should communicate appreciation, not evaluation.

Connection to the 5 How's

The 5 How's are only as honest as the tone that receives their answers. If the leader's tone communicates that the real answer to 'how can this task fail?' should be short and optimistic, the crew will provide short and optimistic answers. Tone determines the quality of information the 5 How's process produces.

Supervisor Toolbox Talk Prompt

Ask your crew this privately and individually: 'On a scale of 1 to 10, how comfortable does it feel to raise a safety concern during a busy day? And what would need to change to make it closer to a 10?' The answers tell you more about your actual safety culture than any metric.

Chapter Summary

- Leadership tone — the emotional climate created by supervisory behavior — is a more powerful determinant of safety behavior than organizational policy.
- Workers calibrate their behavior to the emotional signals of their immediate supervisor, not to formal policy statements.
- Tone change requires behavioral specificity: identifying and practicing the specific behaviors that constitute a welcoming, safety-positive communication style.

- The welcome signal — a visible, consistent behavioral response that communicates genuine appreciation when a worker raises a concern — is one of the most powerful culture-building tools available to a frontline leader.

Leader Action Checklist

[ ] Identify three specific behaviors that make up your welcome signal for safety concerns and practice them deliberately this week.

[ ] Request a behavioral observation from a peer or coach during a representative work period — ask for specific behaviors, not impressions.

[ ] Audit the last five interactions where a worker raised a concern and evaluate your body language and tone in each one.

[ ] Ask one crew member privately this week to rate how comfortable it feels to raise a safety concern — and take the number seriously.

Chapter 12

COACHING VERSUS PUNISHMENT

Leadership Issue

When something goes wrong, an organization reveals what it actually believes about human behavior and how safety is created. If the first response is to identify who made the mistake and assign consequences, the organization communicates that safety is achieved through the threat of punishment. If the first response is to understand what conditions contributed to the mistake and what the system should do differently, the organization communicates that safety is achieved through learning. Both organizations may achieve short-term behavioral change. Only one builds the conditions for long-term improvement.

The Psychology Behind the Risk

Research on reinforcement and learning consistently shows that punishment produces suppression of behavior — the punished behavior decreases in the presence of the punishing stimulus — but does not reliably produce learning, skill development, or changed understanding. In safety contexts, punishment primarily teaches workers what not to do in front of supervisors, not what to understand about risk. It also suppresses reporting: workers who have seen colleagues punished for safety failures learn that the safest personal strategy is to not report their own errors.

Coaching, by contrast, operates through understanding. When a leader helps a worker understand why a condition was hazardous, what decision process produced the behavior, and what different decision process would produce a different outcome, the worker gains something that punishment cannot provide: a mental model that generalizes to new situations. The coached worker handles the next novel hazard better; the punished worker handles the next familiar one less visibly.

Field Example

After a near miss, one supervisor asks who caused it. Another asks what conditions made it possible. The second conversation is longer, more uncomfortable in some ways, and more productive. The first conversation produces an assigned consequence. The second produces an understanding of three system conditions that, unchanged, will produce another event regardless of who is held accountable for this one.

Operational Mechanism

The mechanism of punishment-driven safety is behavioral compliance in the presence of monitoring. Workers do not change their understanding of risk; they change their visible behavior when supervision is active. When monitoring decreases — as it always does — the underlying behavior returns. Coaching-driven safety works through changed understanding, which travels with the worker into every situation, regardless of who is watching.

What Leaders Should Look For

- Workers who follow safety procedures precisely when observed and adapt them when not — the gap between observed and unobserved behavior is a punishment culture indicator.
- Near-miss reporting trends that decline after a disciplinary action — workers are learning that reporting produces punishment.
- Post-incident conversations that end with an assigned consequence but no documented learning about system conditions.
- Workers who describe corrective actions in terms of 'not getting caught' rather than understanding why the behavior was hazardous.
- A pattern where the same types of events recur despite a history of disciplinary actions for previous occurrences.

Leadership Application

Coaching and accountability are not mutually exclusive. The distinction is not between holding people responsible and not holding them responsible — it is about sequencing and purpose. The coaching response to an unsafe act begins with understanding: what happened, what conditions contributed, and what decision process produced the behavior. Accountability comes after understanding and is proportional to the degree to which the behavior was a knowing, willful departure from standards rather than a system-influenced error.

The practical question is: what does this organization want workers to learn from this event? Punishment teaches 'this behavior has consequences.' Coaching teaches 'this is how risk develops, this is what it looks like before something goes wrong, and this is what to do differently.' For most safety incidents, the second lesson is more valuable.

Leadership Development Focus

Supervisors need the skills to conduct a coaching conversation after an unsafe act — which is different from a corrective conversation. The coaching conversation requires suspending judgment long enough to understand the worker's perspective, identifying what decision process produced the behavior, and collaboratively developing an understanding of what would produce a different decision in similar conditions. This requires patience, listening skill, and the ability to separate curiosity about conditions from emotion about the outcome.

Practical Field Integration

Build a 'learning before consequences' practice into your incident response process. Before any corrective action is taken, require a documented answer to three questions: What conditions contributed to this behavior? What did the environment teach this person was acceptable? What system change would make the safer choice easier in the future? Consequence decisions made after this analysis are more accurate and more fair than consequences assigned before it.

Also track the ratio of learning conversations to punitive actions in your incident response. Over time, this ratio should shift toward learning — not because accountability is abandoned, but because most events reveal system conditions that cannot be improved through individual accountability.

Leadership Questions

- After the last unsafe act on my crew, what did the worker learn — and what did the rest of the crew learn from watching the response?
- What does the gap between observed and unobserved behavior on my crew tell me about whether my response builds understanding or compliance?
- Looking at the last five corrective actions in this work area, how many identified system conditions rather than only individual failures?
- What is the impact of my typical incident response on subsequent reporting behavior — does reporting increase or decrease after I respond to an event?
- When a worker makes an error I've seen before, is my first question 'why again?' or 'what conditions made this feel reasonable again?' — and what does that question reveal?

Common Field Traps

- Assuming that consistent accountability for safety violations automatically produces safety improvement — it produces compliance with accountability criteria, which is not the same as learning.
- Treating coaching as a soft alternative to accountability rather than as a different and often more effective path to the same goal: changed behavior.
- Using punishment-based responses for system-influenced errors and wondering why the same events keep recurring.
- Measuring the fairness of consequences without measuring whether they produced learning — accountability without learning is cost without benefit.

- Concluding that a coaching culture means accepting unsafe behavior — coaching responses and clear standards are compatible, and the combination is more effective than either alone.

Prevention Practices

- Implement a 'three questions before consequence' standard: before any corrective action, document answers to 'what conditions contributed?', 'what did the system teach this person was acceptable?', and 'what change would make the safer choice easier?'
- Monitor near-miss reporting trend after every disciplinary action — a reporting decline is evidence that the response taught the wrong lesson.
- Build coaching skills specifically into supervisor development: how to conduct a learning conversation after an unsafe act, not just a corrective one.
- Track recurring incident types and evaluate whether previous accountability responses have produced the learning needed to prevent recurrence.
- Create explicit organizational language about the difference between accountability (appropriate for knowing violations) and coaching (appropriate for system-influenced errors) — so supervisors know which applies when.

Connection to the 5 How's

Coaching naturally aligns with the 5 How's structure. 'How did this condition develop?' and 'How can we prevent it from developing again?' are coaching questions. Using the 5 How's framework in post-incident conversations shifts the discussion from 'who is responsible?' to 'what is the system learning?' — which is the same shift that distinguishes coaching from punishment.

Supervisor Toolbox Talk Prompt

Ask your crew: 'If something went wrong on this task today and you were involved, what would you most be afraid would happen? And what would most help you learn from it?' The answers tell you whether your incident response is producing learning or compliance — and which one will make tomorrow safer.

Chapter Summary

- Punishment teaches workers what not to do in front of supervisors; coaching teaches workers what to understand about risk — only one produces behavior change that travels into unmonitored situations.
- The gap between observed and unobserved behavior on a crew is a direct measure of whether the safety response is building understanding or compliance.
- Coaching and accountability are compatible: the sequence matters — understanding conditions first, then consequence proportional to knowing violation versus system-influenced error.
- Recurring incidents despite a history of disciplinary actions are evidence that the accountability response is not addressing the underlying system conditions.

Leader Action Checklist

[ ] Apply the three questions before consequence standard to your next incident response — document conditions, system learning, and system change before assigning accountability.

[ ] Monitor your near-miss reporting trend for the 30 days following your next corrective action and note whether it increases or decreases.

[ ] Identify one recurring incident type in your work area and evaluate whether previous accountability responses have produced the system learning needed to prevent recurrence.

[ ] Practice one coaching conversation after an unsafe act this month — suspend judgment long enough to understand the decision process before responding.

Chapter 13

TRUST AND PSYCHOLOGICAL SAFETY

Leadership Issue

Trust between leaders and workers is not a morale issue — it is a safety issue. When workers trust their leader, they share what they know, including safety concerns, early warning signs, and honest assessments of risk. When workers do not trust their leader, they share what is safe to share, which in safety-critical environments means they share less than the leader needs to make good decisions. The information environment available to a trusted leader is qualitatively different from the one available to a leader whose crew does not trust them.

The Psychology Behind the Risk

Edmondson (1999) defined psychological safety as 'a belief that the environment is safe for interpersonal risk taking' — specifically, that one will not be punished or humiliated for speaking up, asking questions, or admitting mistakes. Her research found that teams with higher psychological safety learned more from errors, reported more near-misses, and performed better on complex tasks. Critically, she found that psychological safety was not the same as group cohesion or satisfaction — teams could be friendly and still have low psychological safety, and vice versa.

Organizational trust research (Mayer, Davis, & Schoorman, 1995) identifies three components of trust: competence (the trusted party has the ability to do what is needed), benevolence (the trusted party cares about the trusting party's interests), and integrity (the trusted party follows consistent principles). In safety leadership, workers are primarily evaluating whether their leader knows enough to make good safety decisions, whether the leader will protect them when safety and production conflict, and whether the leader's behavior matches their stated values.

Field Example

A crew with trust tells the supervisor the plan is unclear before the work starts. A crew without trust waits, adapts, and works around the confusion silently. Both crews face the same unclear plan. The trusted supervisor gets the information they need to fix it before the task begins. The untrusted supervisor gets a completed task built on improvised solutions they did not know about — and a near-miss report they may never receive.

Operational Mechanism

Trust operates as an information filter. In high-trust environments, relevant safety information flows toward decision-makers. In low-trust environments, the same information is withheld, filtered, or packaged in ways that protect the worker from anticipated negative responses. Leaders making decisions in low-trust environments are making decisions with systematically incomplete information — and they typically do not know it.

What Leaders Should Look For

- Workers who volunteer information about conditions, concerns, and complications without being asked — this is the clearest indicator of functional trust.
- Workers who ask questions that reveal uncertainty or incomplete understanding — willingness to display uncertainty requires trust.
- Pre-task discussions where the crew's plan differs from the written procedure and the supervisor knows about it in advance, rather than discovering it post-event.
- Workers who report their own errors rather than concealing them — this requires trust that errors will be received as learning rather than liability.
- A crew that pushes back on a plan they believe is inadequate rather than executing it silently and hoping it works.

Leadership Application

Trust is built through behavioral consistency over time. Three behaviors are most critical: following through on commitments (integrity), protecting workers when safety and production conflict (benevolence), and demonstrating genuine knowledge of the work (competence). Of these, consistency in the protection behavior — choosing the worker's safety over schedule when the two genuinely conflict — is the most powerful and the hardest to maintain under operational pressure.

Trust can be destroyed much faster than it is built. A single event in which a leader visibly chose production over worker safety, punished someone for raising a concern, or responded to honest reporting with blame can set back trust that took months to establish. Leaders should understand that trust maintenance is not passive — it requires active behavioral consistency even under pressure.

Leadership Development Focus

Supervisors need to understand that trust is not primarily about being liked or having good relationships with their crew — it is about predictable behavior. Workers trust leaders they can predict: leaders whose behavior in safety-production conflicts is consistent and who respond to honest concerns the same way every time, regardless of the operational pressure of the moment. Developing this consistency requires both clarity about personal values and practice maintaining them under pressure.

Practical Field Integration

Build a trust assessment into your leadership self-evaluation. Periodically ask: what has my behavior communicated this week about whether I can be trusted with safety information? Specific behaviors to review include: did I keep a safety commitment I made? Did I protect a worker's safety over schedule when the two conflicted? Did I respond to a concern the same way I would have if the work had not been running behind?

Also build a 'trust temperature check' into your crew relationship: ask one person you trust on the crew to tell you honestly whether the crew feels the leader will protect them if they raise a safety concern that slows the work.

Leadership Questions

- What has my behavior communicated this week about whether I can be trusted with honest safety information?
- When did I last face a clear choice between schedule and a worker's safety, and what did my decision communicate?
- Which workers on my crew consistently share information with me beyond what I ask for — and what is different about my relationship with them?
- If I asked my crew to rate trust from 1 to 10, what number would I hear — and what specific events would they cite to explain it?
- What is the most recent safety commitment I made to my crew, and did I follow through on it visibly?

Common Field Traps

- Confusing being liked with being trusted — a crew can have warm feelings for a leader who they would not trust with a safety concern.
- Building trust in calm periods and inadvertently destroying it in high-pressure ones — trust is most tested, and most formed, when the stakes are highest.
- Treating trust as a fixed property of the relationship rather than as something that is continually built or eroded by specific behaviors.
- Assuming that workers who do not raise concerns with you have no concerns — they may simply not trust that raising them is safe.
- Responding to low trust with more meetings and communication rather than with the specific behavioral changes that trust actually requires.

Prevention Practices

- Build a personal trust behavior standard: identify three specific behaviors you commit to consistently regardless of operational pressure — and evaluate your adherence weekly.
- After any event where you chose production over a worker's safety, evaluate what that choice communicated and what repair action is needed.
- Create a standing 'trust temperature' check with one trusted crew member: ask periodically whether the crew believes you will protect them when safety and schedule conflict.
- Follow through visibly on every safety commitment you make — if a commitment cannot be kept, communicate why and what you will do instead.
- Identify any recent events that may have eroded trust and make a specific behavioral repair, not just a verbal acknowledgment.

Connection to the 5 How's

The quality of answers to 'how can this task fail?' and 'how will controls be verified?' depends directly on the trust level of the relationship between the leader and the crew. Workers who trust their supervisor give honest, complete answers. Workers who do not trust their supervisor give safe answers — answers that will not create problems for them. Trust is the prerequisite for every element of the 5 How's process.

Supervisor Toolbox Talk Prompt

Ask your crew: 'If you noticed today that the plan was not going to work — that conditions had changed and the original approach was going to create a problem — what would you do? Would you stop and tell me, or would you adapt and keep going?' What they say tells you the actual trust level — not the stated one.

Chapter Summary

- Trust is an information-access issue: trusted leaders receive the safety information their crew has; untrusted leaders receive what is safe to share, which is systematically less.
- Trust is built through behavioral consistency in three areas: integrity (following through on commitments), benevolence (protecting workers when safety and production conflict), and competence (knowing the work).
- Trust is destroyed faster than it is built — a single event where a leader chose production over worker safety or punished honest reporting can set back trust built over months.
- Workers who trust their leader will tell them when the plan is wrong before the task starts; workers who do not will adapt and improvise silently — and the leader may never know.

Leader Action Checklist

[ ] Review the last week's behavior: did you keep the safety commitments you made, protect a worker when safety and schedule conflicted, and respond to concerns consistently?

[ ] Ask one trusted crew member privately whether the crew believes you will protect them if they raise a safety concern that slows the work.

[ ] Identify any event in the last month that may have eroded trust and make a specific behavioral repair this week.

[ ] Build a personal trust behavior standard: three specific behaviors you commit to regardless of operational pressure.

Chapter 14

HOW LEADERS ACCIDENTALLY NORMALIZE RISK

Leadership Issue

Most leaders who normalize risk do not know they are doing it. Normalization of deviance — the gradual process by which deviations from standards become accepted as normal — happens through decisions that feel reasonable in the moment: allowing one deviation because the task is almost done, accepting one shortcut because it has worked before, not correcting one discrepancy because more pressing issues exist. No single decision seems significant. The cumulative effect of those decisions is a work environment in which the standard is no longer the actual expectation.

The Psychology Behind the Risk

Diane Vaughan's analysis of the Challenger disaster (1996) introduced the concept of normalization of deviance as an organizational process in which departures from established standards are redefined as acceptable through a series of rationalizations. The O-ring anomalies were present in many previous launches. Each launch without a catastrophic failure became evidence that the anomaly was within acceptable parameters. The standard progressively shifted toward what had been observed, not what had been defined.

In operational environments, normalization operates through the same mechanism: repeated successful outcomes following a deviation teach the system that the deviation is acceptable. Over time, the deviation becomes invisible — it is no longer perceived as a departure from the standard but as part of the standard itself. The leader's silence or inaction at each individual deviation is the mechanism through which this normalization is communicated and reinforced.

Field Example

A supervisor allows an incomplete barricade for a short task. Nothing happens. The next week the same incomplete setup feels acceptable because it already worked once. Three months later, the incomplete barricade is how barricades are set up in this area — not because anyone decided to change the standard, but because the standard was never enforced. The leader's silence taught the workforce that the deviation was acceptable.

Operational Mechanism

The leader's silence in the face of a deviation is not neutral — it is a communication. Workers observe what leaders notice and respond to, and what they do not notice and do not respond to. When a leader consistently does not respond to a specific deviation, the workforce concludes that the deviation is below the response threshold — that it is, effectively, acceptable. Over time, this conclusion becomes the working standard.

What Leaders Should Look For

- Deviations from procedure that have occurred enough times without correction that they no longer prompt comment from anyone on the crew.
- Workers who, when asked about a deviation, reference how long it has been done that way — 'we've always done it like this' or 'nobody has had a problem with it.'
- Documentation of conditions that does not match the observed conditions — what is written as the standard is no longer what is practiced.
- A pattern where the same deviation appears in multiple safety observations without producing a correction or a systemic response.
- Leaders who are aware of a deviation but have rationalized it based on the absence of a previous consequence.

Leadership Application

The most powerful antidote to normalization is consistent response to the first deviation — not the tenth, not when it becomes a trend, but when it first appears. A leader who consistently responds to the first observable departure from standard, even a small one, communicates that the standard is real and that the threshold for response is at the standard, not below it.

This requires leaders to be honest about the deviations they have already normalized — conditions they are aware of but have stopped responding to because of accumulated tolerance. Identifying and correcting those conditions is not just a technical activity; it requires acknowledging that previous silence communicated permission, and that restoring the standard requires explicit communication about why it is being restored.

Leadership Development Focus

Supervisors need to develop awareness of their own normalization — the conditions they have been aware of but have not responded to, and the rationalizations they have used to justify inaction. This is uncomfortable territory because it requires honestly examining the gap between a leader's stated standards and their actual response patterns. Development conversations that explore this gap specifically — without assigning blame — are among the most valuable supervision development experiences.

Practical Field Integration

Build a normalization audit into your quarterly leadership review. Pull the last three months of safety observations and identify any conditions that appeared more than once without a documented correction. These repeat observations are normalization indicators: the condition was noticed but not corrected, which means the standard was observed but not enforced.

Also build a 'first deviation response' standard into your leadership behavior: when you observe a departure from a clear standard, respond at the first observation, not after a pattern has established itself.

Leadership Questions

- What conditions exist in my work area that I am aware of but have not corrected — and what rationalization am I using to justify that inaction?
- Looking at repeat safety observations, what conditions have been noted multiple times without a systemic correction?
- Where has my silence at a deviation communicated permission — and how do I correct that communication now?
- What was the last clear standard departure I observed, and how quickly did I respond — and what did the response speed teach the crew?
- If I compared the current working practices in my area to the documented procedures, where would I find the largest gap?

Common Field Traps

- Using the absence of a previous incident as evidence that a deviation is acceptable — the absence of a consequence does not validate a departure from standard.
- Normalizing deviations that 'everyone does' rather than evaluating them against the written standard — universal practice does not make a deviation safe.
- Delaying response to a deviation until it becomes a pattern, by which time the normalization is already established.
- Treating normalization as a worker issue rather than as a leadership failure — normalization requires leadership inaction to persist.
- Confusing the practical adaptation of experienced workers with the gradual erosion of necessary standards — these are different things that look similar from the outside.

Prevention Practices

- Build a 'first deviation response' standard: commit to responding at the first observable departure from a clear standard, not after a pattern establishes itself.

- Conduct a quarterly normalization audit: pull safety observations for repeat items and evaluate whether each was corrected at the system level.
- Conduct a personal normalization review: identify conditions you are aware of but have not corrected, and evaluate the rationalizations you have used.
- Compare current documented procedure to current observed practice at least twice per year — the gap between the two is the normalization measure.
- When restoring a standard that has drifted, communicate explicitly with the crew about why the change is being made — silence about the change teaches only the new enforcement, not the reasoning behind it.

Connection to the 5 How's

'How should this task be performed?' has a definitive answer: the documented procedure. 'How can this task fail?' includes failure through normalized deviation. Using the 5 How's creates a regular opportunity to compare current practice to established standard — and to catch normalization before it produces an incident.

Supervisor Toolbox Talk Prompt

Ask your crew: 'Looking at how we're actually doing this task today versus how the procedure says to do it — what are the differences? And for each difference, help me understand: is this an improvement on the procedure, or is this a shortcut that's become normal?' This conversation surfaces normalization directly.

Chapter Summary

- Normalization of deviance is a leadership failure, not a worker failure — it requires supervisory inaction at each individual deviation to persist.
- Repeated successful outcomes following a deviation are the mechanism by which the deviation is redefined as acceptable — the absence of a consequence does not validate a departure from standard.

- The most powerful antidote to normalization is consistent response to the first deviation — before a pattern establishes itself and before rationalization becomes entrenched.
- A normalization audit — comparing documented procedure to observed practice and identifying repeat observations without systemic correction — is a reliable tool for identifying where standards have drifted.

Leader Action Checklist

[ ] Identify one condition you have been aware of but have not corrected — evaluate the rationalization you are using and decide whether it holds up.

[ ] Pull the last three months of safety observations and identify any condition that appeared more than once without a documented systemic correction.

[ ] Compare the documented procedure for one high-risk task to the current observed practice and identify where the gaps are.

[ ] Commit to the first deviation response standard for one specific safety requirement this week and document your response.

PART III — PREVENTIVE SAFETY LEADERSHIP

Prevention requires more than knowledge of hazards and procedures. It requires a specific set of leadership capabilities: the emotional intelligence to build trust and manage the human side of safety conversations, the cognitive discipline to look for what could go wrong rather than confirming that everything is fine, and the cultural understanding to shape an environment where preventive thinking is the norm rather than the exception. Part III develops these capabilities.

Chapter 15

EMOTIONAL INTELLIGENCE IN SAFETY LEADERSHIP

Leadership Issue

Emotional intelligence in safety leadership is not about being pleasant or avoiding conflict. It is about the ability to read and manage emotional conditions — one's own and others' — in ways that keep safety-critical communication functioning even when conditions are difficult. A leader with high emotional intelligence maintains the communication channel under stress, recognizes when someone's emotional state is affecting their judgment, and navigates difficult safety conversations without triggering the defensive responses that shut down honest information exchange.

The Psychology Behind the Risk

Goleman's framework for emotional intelligence (1995) identifies five domains: self-awareness, self-regulation, motivation, empathy, and social skill. In safety leadership, self-awareness and empathy are the most operationally critical. Self-awareness — the ability to recognize one's own emotional state and its effect on behavior — allows leaders to manage the impact of their emotional state on the crew's communication environment. Empathy — the ability to understand others' emotional experience — allows leaders to recognize when a worker's emotional state is affecting their safety behavior and to respond appropriately.

Neuroscience research on emotional regulation shows that the ability to regulate emotional responses under stress is a learnable skill — one that improves with deliberate practice and degrades without it. Leaders who develop deliberate regulation practices perform better under the specific conditions that safety leadership requires: high stakes, time pressure, conflicting demands, and the need to maintain clear communication while managing one's own stress.

Field Example

A frustrated leader corrects a worker publicly and the crew becomes silent. The correction was technically accurate — the behavior needed to change. But the emotional execution produced defensive responses across the crew that will suppress safety communication for the rest of the shift. Another leader pauses, asks what happened, corrects the issue privately, and ends with the crew's communication channel intact.

Operational Mechanism

Emotional intelligence creates what might be called 'emotional headroom' — the psychological space in which difficult safety conversations can happen without triggering defensive responses. When this headroom is absent, accurate safety information gets filtered through emotional self-protection: workers say what is safe rather than what is accurate, concerns are withheld to avoid conflict, and honest assessments of risk are suppressed to avoid the emotional cost of raising them.

What Leaders Should Look For

- Workers who visibly relax when a specific supervisor is present and become more guarded when another arrives — tracking which leaders create emotional headroom and which reduce it.

- Difficult safety conversations that end without resolution because the emotional temperature prevented honest exchange.
- A leader whose stress is visibly affecting the crew's communication quality — tighter posture, shorter answers, reduced questioning.
- Workers who avoid informing a leader about a developing problem because of the anticipated emotional response.
- Post-task accounts where workers say they 'didn't want to add to the pressure' by raising a concern.

Leadership Application

The highest-leverage emotional intelligence skill for safety leaders is what might be called 'emotional de-escalation before information gathering.' When something has gone wrong, the leader's first emotional response — typically some version of concern, frustration, or urgency — will determine whether workers give honest accounts or protective ones. A leader who visibly regulates their emotional response before asking questions creates the conditions for more accurate information.

The practical tool is the pause before the question: after an unsafe act or near-miss, take a deliberate breath, regulate visibly, and begin with an information question rather than a reactive statement. 'Walk me through what happened from your perspective' produces different information than any statement that begins with emotional content.

Leadership Development Focus

Supervisors need to develop emotional intelligence specifically in the context of safety leadership rather than in generic interpersonal situations. The relevant skill is not managing emotions in comfortable conditions — it is maintaining emotional regulation under the specific stressors that safety leadership involves: discovering that a safety standard was not followed, receiving a near-miss report for a serious event, managing a crew that is behind schedule and taking shortcuts. Practice must occur under conditions that resemble these situations.

Practical Field Integration

Build a post-difficult-conversation debrief into your leadership routine. After any safety conversation that involved emotional complexity — a correction, a near-miss discussion, a plan disagreement — ask yourself: what was my emotional state, how did it affect my communication, and what do I need to do differently next time? This reflection builds the self-awareness that makes emotional regulation possible.

Also build a standing practice of asking, after receiving any safety concern, 'What was the emotional cost of raising that concern for the person who raised it?' — and ensuring that the response reduced rather than increased that cost.

Leadership Questions

- When I receive a safety concern or discover an unsafe act, what is my first emotional response, and what does that response communicate to the person delivering the information?
- Which of my emotional reactions under operational pressure most reliably reduces the quality of safety communication in my crew?
- What does my crew's behavior tell me about whether I am creating emotional headroom — the psychological space in which difficult safety conversations can happen?
- When was the last time I regulated a difficult emotional response in a safety conversation — and what did that regulation make possible?
- What would an emotionally intelligent response look like to the last difficult safety situation I faced — and how close did my actual response come to that?

Common Field Traps

- Confusing emotional suppression with emotional regulation — leaders who suppress emotion under stress are not managing it, and it will emerge in other ways.
- Treating emotional intelligence as a soft skill unrelated to operational outcomes, when research consistently shows it determines the quality of safety communication.
- Applying emotional intelligence only to individual interactions while missing its effect on the crew's overall communication environment.
- Using technical competence as a substitute for emotional regulation — a leader who is right about the safety issue but wrong in the emotional execution still damages the communication environment.
- Developing emotional intelligence in training contexts that do not resemble the specific stressors of safety leadership, producing skills that do not transfer.

Prevention Practices

- Build a standing pause-before-question practice for safety conversations following unsafe acts: regulate emotional state before gathering information.
- Develop a post-conversation debrief habit: after any emotionally complex safety conversation, ask what emotional state you brought in and how it affected the information exchange.
- Identify your highest-impact emotional trigger in safety leadership contexts and develop a specific regulation practice for that trigger.
- Ask a trusted colleague or crew member periodically to describe the emotional headroom available in your work environment — not whether you are a good person, but whether difficult safety conversations can happen.
- Practice the empathy question after any safety concern is raised: 'What was the emotional cost of raising this for the person who raised it?' — and reduce that cost where possible.

Connection to the 5 How's

Emotional intelligence is the prerequisite for 5 How's conversations that produce honest answers. Workers who do not feel emotionally safe giving honest answers to 'how can this task fail?' will give brief, optimistic, socially acceptable answers. Leaders who have developed the emotional intelligence to create that safety will receive the information the 5 How's are designed to surface.

Supervisor Toolbox Talk Prompt

Reflect on this privately and then share what you're willing to: 'Think of a time when you knew something was wrong but didn't say it because of how you thought the response would feel. What would it have taken to say it? And what can I do differently to make that conversation easier?' This is among the most revealing conversations a leader can have with their crew.

Chapter Summary

- Emotional intelligence in safety leadership is not about being pleasant — it is about maintaining the emotional conditions under which accurate safety information can be communicated.
- The leader's emotional response to a safety concern or unsafe act determines whether workers give honest accounts or protective ones — emotional regulation before information gathering is the key skill.
- Emotional headroom — the psychological space in which difficult safety conversations can happen — is created and maintained by specific, learnable leader behaviors.
- Emotional intelligence skills that are developed in generic interpersonal contexts must be specifically practiced under the stressors of safety leadership to transfer to those situations.

Leader Action Checklist

[ ] Build the pause-before-question practice into your next response to an unsafe act or safety concern — regulate emotional state before gathering information.

[ ] Debrief one emotionally complex safety conversation this week: what was your emotional state, how did it affect communication, and what would you do differently?

[ ] Ask a trusted colleague to describe the emotional headroom in your work environment — whether difficult safety conversations can happen.

[ ] Identify your most impactful emotional trigger in safety conversations and develop one specific regulation practice for it.

Chapter 16

THE PSYCHOLOGY OF SHORTCUTS

Leadership Issue

Shortcuts are not primarily a motivation or attitude problem. They are a rationalization problem. Workers who take shortcuts in safety-critical tasks have almost always constructed a cognitive justification for why the shortcut is acceptable — why it does not really matter in this case, why the risk is lower than the procedure implies, or why the task is different enough from the scenario the procedure was written for that the procedure's requirements do not fully apply. Understanding the rationalization is more useful for prevention than understanding the shortcut itself.

The Psychology Behind the Risk

Kahneman's distinction between System 1 (fast, intuitive, automatic) and System 2 (slow, deliberate, analytical) thinking (2011) provides a framework for understanding shortcut psychology. Shortcuts represent System 1 behavior replacing System 2 requirements. When a worker takes a shortcut on a complex task, they are running a fast, intuitive response where the situation requires deliberate analysis. This substitution often feels like efficiency rather than risk-taking, because System 1 processing is experienced as fluent and confident.

Rationalization research shows that people construct post-hoc justifications for decisions that were made on non-rational grounds. A worker who skips a verification step because they are in a hurry will typically construct a plausible reason why the verification was not necessary in this case — 'the last inspection was clean,' 'this equipment has never had an issue,' 'I can tell by looking that it's fine.' These rationalizations are sincere; the worker is not lying. They are a natural cognitive response to the dissonance between taking a shortcut and believing oneself to be a safe worker.

Field Example

A team skips a verification step because the paperwork feels repetitive and no issue has ever been found. The rationalization is genuine: the step has never found a problem, so it feels like administrative overhead rather than protective control. The shortcut feels efficient. It continues until conditions change — equipment ages, a different operator, a new failure mode — and the verification step would have found the problem that the shortcut missed.

Operational Mechanism

Shortcuts are reinforced by success. Every time a shortcut works — every time the skipped verification reveals nothing retroactively important — the brain updates its probability estimate: this verification is not worth its cost. Over many repetitions, the verification step is mentally re-categorized from protective control to administrative burden. The step does not disappear; it is downgraded to something that can be done perfunctorily rather than genuinely.

What Leaders Should Look For

- Workers who can fluently explain why a specific procedural step is 'not necessary in this case' — the fluency of the justification indicates practiced rationalization.
- Verification steps that are completed faster than the procedure allows — indicating they are being executed as a formality rather than a genuine check.
- Tasks where the documentation is always clean but field conditions vary — suggesting that documentation has become separate from actual verification.
- Workers who are surprised when a verification step actually finds a problem — their surprise reveals that the step had been categorized as a formality.
- Shortcuts that are consistent across the crew, indicating they are established practice rather than individual improvisation.

Leadership Application

The response to shortcuts requires engaging the rationalization, not just the behavior. Telling a worker to follow the procedure does not address the rationalization that made the shortcut feel acceptable — it simply reestablishes compliance through authority, which persists only while the authority is present.

The more effective conversation engages the rationalization directly: 'I understand why this step feels unnecessary — it's never found a problem in recent memory. Help me think through what would change if conditions were different, and whether the step would still matter in that scenario.' This approach respects the worker's cognitive experience while building a more accurate risk model.

Leadership Development Focus

Supervisors need to develop the ability to identify the rationalization pattern behind a shortcut, not just the shortcut itself. Different rationalization patterns require different responses: 'this step has never found anything' requires a conversation about low-frequency, high-consequence events; 'everyone does it this way' requires a conversation about normalization and collective risk; 'this task is different from the one the procedure was written for' requires a genuine evaluation of whether the procedure needs to be updated or whether the reasoning is post-hoc justification.

Practical Field Integration

Build a verification quality check into your safety observations. Rather than simply confirming that verification steps were completed, evaluate whether they were completed as genuine checks: did the worker pause, look, confirm, and then proceed? Or did they execute the paperwork while already mentally committed to the next step? The difference between a genuine verification and a performed one is observable.

Also create a standing conversation about rationalization culture: normalize asking 'what's the reasoning behind this shortcut?' as a learning question rather than an accusatory one.

Leadership Questions

- What is the standard rationalization my crew uses for the most common shortcut in this work area — and how would I engage that rationalization in conversation?
- Which verification steps in our operation have been mentally re-categorized as administrative burden rather than genuine protective controls — and what produced that re-categorization?
- What would it take for a worker on this crew to discover that a verification step actually matters — and is our current approach giving them that experience?
- When was the last time a verification step in this area found a genuine problem, and does the crew know about it?
- What does the quality of verification behavior in this crew tell me about whether those steps are being treated as controls or as overhead?

Common Field Traps

- Addressing shortcut behavior through repeated compliance reminders without engaging the rationalization — compliance enforcement changes behavior in the presence of monitoring but does not change the cognitive model that produced the behavior.
- Treating a shortcut as evidence of poor attitude when it is more often evidence of a well-developed rationalization that the leader has not yet engaged.
- Missing the difference between a genuine verification and a performed one — a worker who executes a checklist item while mentally committed to the next step is not verifying.
- Allowing successful outcomes following shortcuts to go uncommented — silence after a successful shortcut communicates permission.

- Developing rationalization patterns — the specific justifications workers use for specific shortcuts — as operational intelligence rather than tracking them only as procedure violations.

Prevention Practices

- Build verification quality checks into your observations: evaluate whether verification steps are being executed as genuine checks or as performed formalities.
- Engage the rationalization behind each major shortcut you observe — understand the cognitive justification before responding to the behavior.
- Create regular reminders of what verification steps have historically found — making the protective value visible reduces the re-categorization to administrative burden.
- Build a 'last time this step found something' awareness into crew knowledge for your highest-risk verification steps.
- Address new shortcuts at first appearance, before the rationalization becomes practiced and before the shortcut becomes crew-normal.

Connection to the 5 How's

'How can this task fail?' specifically targets the rationalizations that produce shortcuts: 'it's never failed before' is an answer to 'how can this fail?' that the 5 How's framework can challenge by asking what conditions would have to change for the failure to become possible. Used consistently, this question builds the habit of reasoning beyond previous successful outcomes.

Supervisor Toolbox Talk Prompt

Ask your crew: 'In this task, what's the step that's most likely to get done quickly or skipped? Not because people don't care — but because it usually doesn't find anything and it feels like overhead. Now let's talk about what that step is actually protecting against and what conditions would make it matter.'

Chapter Summary

- Shortcuts are a rationalization problem, not primarily a motivation problem — workers construct sincere cognitive justifications for why a shortcut is acceptable in their specific situation.
- Shortcuts are reinforced by success: every time a skipped step reveals nothing retroactively important, the brain updates its probability estimate and the step is further downgraded.
- Addressing shortcuts requires engaging the rationalization, not just the behavior — compliance enforcement changes visible behavior but does not change the cognitive model.
- Verification quality — the difference between a genuine check and a performed formality — is observable and tells leaders whether protective steps are functioning as controls.

Leader Action Checklist

[ ] Identify the most common shortcut in your work area and document the standard rationalization used to justify it.

[ ] Conduct a verification quality observation this week: evaluate whether steps are being executed as genuine checks or performed formalities.

[ ] Create awareness among the crew of what the most important verification steps have historically found — make their protective value visible.

[ ] Practice engaging a rationalization this week: when you observe a shortcut, ask about the reasoning before responding to the behavior.

Chapter 17

WHY PEOPLE IGNORE WEAK SIGNALS

Leadership Issue

Most serious incidents are preceded by weak signals — small indicators that something in the system is drifting or degrading. These signals are typically visible to someone in the organization before the incident occurs. The question is not whether they existed, but why they were not recognized, escalated, or acted upon. Understanding how weak signals get filtered out — individually and organizationally — is one of the most important capabilities in preventive safety leadership.

The Psychology Behind the Risk

Signal detection theory, developed in the context of radar operations (Green & Swets, 1966) and later applied to medical and safety contexts, describes the challenge of distinguishing meaningful signals from background noise. In operational environments, weak signals are difficult to act on because the base rate of false alarms is high: most minor equipment issues do not precede major failures, most communication gaps do not precede incidents, most small deviations do not precede serious events. The statistical challenge of identifying the real signal in a noisy environment creates a legitimate cognitive burden for leaders.

Organizational filters compound the problem. Weick and Sutcliffe (2001) identify the failure to 'be sensitive to operations' as a primary cause of high-reliability failures: organizations that focus on outcomes (injuries, incidents) rather than process indicators (near-misses, weak signals, communication quality) are systematically blind to the early indicators that precede serious events. Leadership attention and organizational reporting systems that focus only on lagging indicators create a culture in which weak signals are not valued as information.

Field Example

A minor equipment issue, a repeated communication gap, and declining housekeeping each appear small individually. Separately, each is easily explained away. Together, they indicate a system losing discipline — a pattern that is visible in aggregate but invisible when each piece is evaluated in isolation. The aggregated signal was available; no one aggregated it.

Operational Mechanism

Weak signals are filtered through three mechanisms: cognitive dismissal (the signal doesn't seem significant enough to act on), organizational dilution (the signal is reported but not escalated or aggregated), and rationalization (the signal is explained by a local cause that doesn't implicate a systemic issue). All three mechanisms can be present simultaneously, and all three operate more powerfully under time pressure and workload.

What Leaders Should Look For

- Repeated minor issues of the same type — the same equipment, the same process step, the same communication gap — that are being addressed individually but not as a pattern.
- Near-miss reports that describe a local cause without examining what system conditions created the opportunity for the near-miss.
- Indicators in adjacent systems — housekeeping quality, tool organization, documentation accuracy — that have declined without investigation.
- Workers who have noticed something 'off' but have not reported it because it 'isn't bad enough' to report.
- A gap between the number of small issues the crew is aware of and the number that have been formally reported or investigated.

Leadership Application

Weak signal management requires two capabilities: pattern recognition (the ability to see the aggregate picture from individual data points) and threshold calibration (knowing what level of signal warrants escalation or investigation). Most organizations calibrate their threshold to the individual signal level rather than the pattern level, which means systemic degradation can accumulate without crossing the threshold at any single point.

Leaders who develop weak signal sensitivity ask a different question about each minor event: not 'is this significant enough to act on?' but 'what does this tell me about the state of the system?' The second question evaluates each signal as evidence about the whole rather than as an isolated event requiring a local response.

Leadership Development Focus

Supervisors need to develop the habit of aggregating minor signals into a systemic picture rather than addressing each one in isolation. This requires building a simple tracking practice: when the same type of issue occurs more than twice in a period, treat it as a pattern indicator requiring systemic investigation regardless of the severity of each individual instance.

Practical Field Integration

Implement a weak signal review as a standing element of your weekly leadership review. Collect three categories of minor indicators — near-misses and close calls, repeat observations of the same issue, and indicators in adjacent systems like housekeeping and documentation — and evaluate them in aggregate. The aggregate picture almost always shows something that individual review misses.

Also create a low-threshold reporting expectation: normalize reporting signals that are 'not quite a near-miss' — things workers noticed that seemed slightly off but did not produce an event. These are often the most valuable signals in the system.

Leadership Questions

- What minor issues have occurred more than twice in the last 90 days — and have they been investigated as a pattern or addressed individually?
- What is the quality of adjacent indicators — housekeeping, documentation accuracy, communication quality — compared to 90 days ago?
- What concerns have workers expressed informally that have not been formally reported because they 'weren't bad enough'?
- What does the aggregate picture of all minor signals in the last quarter tell me that individual investigation of each signal did not?
- Where in our reporting system do weak signals get diluted — what happens to a signal between when a worker notices it and when a leader acts on it?

Common Field Traps

- Addressing each weak signal as an isolated event rather than as evidence about the state of the system.
- Setting reporting thresholds that exclude the weakest signals — which are often the most valuable for preventive analysis.
- Using lagging indicators (injuries, incidents) as the primary evidence of safety system health, which provides a picture of what has already gone wrong rather than what is developing.
- Assuming that minor issues that have been 'fixed' locally have been addressed — local correction of a symptom without investigation of the cause leaves the pattern intact.
- Undervaluing informal worker observations because they are not formal reports — informal observations often carry weak signals that formal systems are not designed to capture.

Prevention Practices

- Implement a pattern threshold rule: when any issue type appears more than twice in a period, investigate it as a systemic indicator regardless of individual severity.

- Create a low-threshold reporting expectation: explicitly invite reporting of 'things that seemed slightly off' rather than only reportable events.
- Build a weekly aggregate review of minor signals — near-misses, repeat observations, adjacent indicators — and evaluate the picture they collectively create.
- Track the ratio of informal worker observations to formal reports and investigate significant gaps — signals being discussed but not recorded indicate a reporting threshold problem.
- Develop your own pattern recognition practice: when you receive any minor report, ask first 'what is this one instance telling me about the state of the larger system?'

Connection to the 5 How's

'How will we know the controls are working?' is the 5 How's question that most directly addresses weak signals. Answering this question honestly requires leaders to think about what an early indicator of control failure looks like — which is exactly the weak signal question. Building this into every pre-task discussion builds the habit of watching for weak signals as part of normal task execution.

Supervisor Toolbox Talk Prompt

Ask your crew: 'Before we start — and I mean this as a real question — is there anything about this task, this equipment, or this environment that has seemed slightly off lately? Not a reportable incident, but something that made you think or gave you a brief moment of concern? What was it?' The responses to this question are often the most valuable safety intelligence you'll collect all week.

Chapter Summary

- Weak signals precede most serious incidents — the challenge is not their absence but the cognitive and organizational filters that prevent them from being recognized and aggregated.

- Individual signal evaluation misses patterns that aggregate signal review reveals — the same minor issue occurring multiple times is a different kind of information than one occurrence.
- Low-threshold reporting — creating a standing invitation for workers to report things that 'seemed slightly off' — is one of the highest-value practices in preventive safety leadership.
- Adjacent indicators — housekeeping quality, documentation accuracy, communication patterns — are among the most sensitive early indicators of system degradation.

Leader Action Checklist

[ ] Review the last 90 days of minor reports and observations for any issue type that has appeared more than twice — and investigate as a pattern.

[ ] Implement a standing 'slightly off' question in your next toolbox talk and document what the crew reports.

[ ] Evaluate adjacent indicators this week: housekeeping, documentation quality, and communication patterns compared to 90 days ago.

[ ] Check whether your current reporting threshold is excluding weak signals that workers are noticing but not formally reporting.

Chapter 18

THE MENTAL DRIFT TOWARD EXPOSURE

Leadership Issue

Drift is the process by which a safe operation gradually becomes a less safe one, through a series of small decisions, adaptations, and compromises that each seem reasonable in isolation. Organizations do not typically choose to become less safe. They drift there, one apparently reasonable accommodation at a time. The challenge for safety leaders is that drift is inherently difficult to see from inside the process — each individual step away from the established standard feels like a reasonable response to current conditions, and the distance from the original standard is only visible in aggregate.

The Psychology Behind the Risk

Rasmussen's risk management model (1997) describes a 'migration toward the boundary of acceptable performance' as a natural organizational process: operations drift toward the boundary between safe and unsafe because short-term efficiencies accumulate, controls are simplified, and the pressure to reduce cost and complexity is persistent. Unless active counterpressure is applied, drift toward less safe conditions is the natural direction of organizational evolution.

Dekker's (2011) work on 'drift into failure' extends this by describing how normal work — the continuous adaptation of procedures to local conditions, the optimization of routines, the simplification of controls that seem redundant — is the mechanism of drift, not an aberration from it. Drift does not require bad decisions. It requires only the accumulation of locally reasonable ones in the absence of adequate systemic oversight.

Field Example

Temporary overtime, rushed turnover, and informal workarounds begin as short-term fixes for a specific operational period. Three months later, they are part of how the work is done. No one decided to make them permanent. They became permanent through the absence of a decision to eliminate them. The drift was gradual, each step was explained by something real, and the distance from the original standard became visible only when measured against it.

Operational Mechanism

Drift is powered by the accumulation of individually rational decisions and the absence of aggregate review. Each small adaptation makes sense given the specific conditions that produced it. The pattern that emerges from many such adaptations — a progressive departure from safety standards — is only visible to someone who is comparing current practice to an established baseline, not to someone inside the adaptations making the next one.

What Leaders Should Look For

- Temporary measures — overtime, workarounds, modified procedures — that have been in place for more than 30 days without a plan for resolution.
- Procedures that are written one way but have been informally modified across the crew without a formal procedure change.
- A difference between how a task is described in onboarding documents and how it is actually performed by experienced workers.
- Crew members who cannot articulate when or why a specific practice changed from the documented procedure.
- The sense, in periodic procedure reviews, that the review is documenting what is currently done rather than evaluating whether what is currently done is what was intended.

Leadership Application

The most reliable tool against drift is periodic baseline comparison – deliberately measuring current practice against the standard from which it has drifted, rather than comparing current practice to recent practice. A leader who measures current practice only against what was normal last month will not see gradual drift; a leader who measures against the documented standard will.

This requires leaders to take documented procedures seriously as a reference point rather than treating them as guidelines that experienced workers have evolved beyond. When current practice has genuinely improved on the procedure, the improvement should be documented. When it has departed from the procedure for reasons of convenience or pressure, that departure should be identified and addressed.

Leadership Development Focus

Supervisors need to develop the habit of measuring practice against documented standards rather than against recent history. This requires a different orientation toward procedures: not as bureaucratic artifacts that experienced workers have moved beyond, but as the established best thinking about how to do the work safely, which should be explicitly improved or explicitly followed.

Practical Field Integration

Build a drift assessment into your quarterly review. Choose three high-risk tasks and compare how they are currently being performed to how the procedure documents they should be performed. For each difference, evaluate: is this a genuine improvement that should be formalized, or a drift from standard that should be corrected?

Also build a temporal comparison into your routine: how does this task look today compared to how it looked six months ago? The temporal comparison catches drift that baseline comparison misses when the baseline itself has drifted.

Leadership Questions

- What temporary measures, workarounds, or informal adaptations are currently in use in this operation, and when were they introduced as temporary?
- If I compared how high-risk tasks are currently performed to how the documented procedure says they should be performed, what would I find?
- What has changed in this operation over the last six months — in practice, not in procedure — and is each change an improvement or a drift?
- Which conditions that exist today would not have been acceptable 12 months ago — and what produced the change in acceptability?
- Where is there a difference between what experienced workers do and what the onboarding training teaches — and which one is right?

Common Field Traps

- Comparing current practice to recent practice rather than to documented standard — this makes gradual drift invisible by renormalizing the comparison point.
- Treating informal worker adaptations as proof of experience rather than as potential evidence of drift — experience-based adaptations and drift can look identical.
- Allowing procedure reviews to become documentation of current practice rather than evaluation of whether current practice is adequate.
- Treating temporary measures as closed issues once the immediate pressure passes — temporary measures that are not explicitly eliminated become permanent through default.
- Using the absence of incidents as evidence that the current practice level is adequate — drift produces incidents only at the end of a long process.

Prevention Practices

- Build a quarterly drift assessment into your leadership review: compare three high-risk tasks to their documented procedures and evaluate each difference.
- Establish a 30-day rule for temporary measures: any temporary adaptation in place for more than 30 days requires a formal decision about whether it should be formalized or eliminated.
- Build temporal comparison into your observation practice: when observing a task, ask how it compares to six months ago rather than only to recent practice.
- Conduct an annual procedure-versus-practice review for all high-risk tasks and formally update procedures where practice has genuinely improved, and correct practice where it has drifted.
- Create a specific organizational trigger for drift review after any sustained period of elevated pressure — after a push, after an overtime period, after a period of resource constraint — because these periods reliably produce drift.

Connection to the 5 How's

'How should this task be performed?' is the anti-drift question. Answering it honestly requires consulting the documented procedure rather than relying on current practice memory. When the 5 How's are used consistently, this question periodically surfaces the difference between what the procedure says and what the crew is actually doing — which is the drift measurement.

Supervisor Toolbox Talk Prompt

Ask your crew: 'Compare how we do this task today to how we did it 12 months ago. What has changed? For each change — is it something we decided to change because it was better, or is it something that just gradually became how we do it without anyone making that decision?' The second category is drift.

Chapter Summary

- Drift is the natural direction of operational evolution in the absence of active counterpressure — each individual step seems reasonable while the cumulative departure from standard becomes dangerous.
- Drift is invisible from inside the process: it requires comparison to a stable baseline, not to recent practice, to become visible.
- Temporary measures that are not explicitly eliminated become permanent through default — the absence of a decision to reverse them is a decision to keep them.
- Periodic baseline comparison — measuring current practice against documented standards rather than against recent history — is the most reliable tool for detecting and correcting drift.

Leader Action Checklist

[ ] Identify any temporary measures, workarounds, or informal adaptations currently in use that have been in place for more than 30 days.

[ ] Compare how one high-risk task is currently performed to its documented procedure and evaluate each difference: improvement or drift?

[ ] Ask your crew how the three most common tasks have changed over the last 12 months — and evaluate whether the changes were decided or drifted.

[ ] Build a 30-day rule for temporary measures: any adaptation still in place at 30 days requires a formal decision about its status.

Chapter 19

CURIOSITY AS A PREVENTIVE LEADERSHIP SKILL

Leadership Issue

The reflexive response to a safety problem — who did this, what rule was violated, what consequence applies — is not a curious response. It is an evaluative one. Evaluation-first safety leadership produces defensiveness, limited information, and surface-level corrections. Curiosity-first safety leadership produces better information, more honest accounts, and more accurate understanding of why things happen. Developing genuine curiosity as a leadership posture is one of the highest-leverage investments a safety leader can make.

The Psychology Behind the Risk

Inquiry-based leadership research consistently shows that leaders who ask genuine questions — who do not know the answer before they ask and who listen to be informed rather than to confirm — receive qualitatively different and more useful information than leaders who ask questions to establish fault or demonstrate knowledge. The difference is perceptible to the person being asked: they can tell the difference between a genuine inquiry and an interrogation, and they respond to each differently.

Baumeister and Leary's research on belongingness and social acceptance (1995) provides context: workers who are asked genuine questions by a leader experience the interaction as relationally positive — as evidence that the leader is interested in their perspective. This relational positive is itself a trust-building event, independent of the content of the answer. Leaders who develop genuine curiosity build trust as a byproduct of asking honest questions.

Field Example

A leader asks why employees are avoiding a process rather than simply demanding compliance. The answer reveals the process is difficult to use under field conditions — the form is designed for an office environment, not a noisy one; the required information is not visible from where workers are positioned; the sequence of steps does not match the sequence of the task. The curiosity revealed the actual reason, which was operational, not motivational.

Operational Mechanism

Curiosity works by suspending the evaluative conclusion long enough to gather more accurate information. The evaluative reflex — this is wrong, who is responsible, what consequence applies — produces a short, efficient process that generates incomplete understanding. Curiosity delays the conclusion long enough to understand the conditions, and that delay is where the most valuable safety learning happens.

What Leaders Should Look For

- Leaders who ask 'why' before they ask 'who' when something goes wrong — this ordering reveals a curiosity-first orientation.
- Post-incident conversations that produce operational insights rather than only assigned consequences — the depth of insight indicates whether curiosity was present.
- Workers who describe their leader's response to problems as 'actually listening' rather than as 'waiting to respond' — this distinction indicates the presence of genuine inquiry.
- Leaders who change their operational understanding as a result of a safety conversation — if the leader's position never changes, the questions were not genuine.
- A culture where workers anticipate being asked about their perspective rather than being told what they did wrong.

Leadership Application

Developing curiosity as a practice requires replacing specific reflexive responses with specific curious alternatives. The reflexive 'why did you do that?' (interrogative, tone of accusation) becomes 'walk me through your thinking' (genuinely interested in the decision process). The reflexive 'you know the procedure' (compliance reminder) becomes 'what made the procedure feel like it didn't quite fit this situation?' (genuinely interested in the operational context).

These replacements require practice because the reflexive responses are stronger than the curious ones — they are faster, more familiar, and reinforced by years of authority-based interaction habits. Curiosity under pressure is a developed skill, not a natural default for most people with supervisory authority.

Leadership Development Focus

Supervisors need to develop the specific skill of asking questions they don't know the answer to, in safety contexts where they have the authority to evaluate and correct. This is cognitively and socially harder than it sounds: a supervisor asking 'what made you decide to do it that way?' when they know how it should have been done is practicing genuine curiosity in a context where evaluation is the expected mode. This requires deliberate practice with feedback.

Practical Field Integration

Build a curiosity moment into your post-task debrief routine. After every task of moderate or higher risk, ask one genuinely open question — one you do not know the answer to — and listen to the response. This does not have to be lengthy: 'What do you know about that task now that you didn't know before we started?' takes thirty seconds and produces better operational intelligence than most formal debriefs.

Also track your own question types: what proportion of the questions you ask in safety conversations are genuine inquiries versus evaluative questions (where you already know what answer you're looking for)?

Leadership Questions

- In the last safety conversation I had following an unsafe act, how many of my questions were genuine inquiries versus questions designed to lead to the conclusion I had already reached?
- What is the most important thing I do not understand about how and why a specific unsafe behavior occurs in my work area — and what question would I need to ask to find out?
- What would my crew tell me about this work environment if they believed I was genuinely curious rather than evaluating them?
- When a worker does something that seems unreasonable to me, what question would help me understand why it seemed reasonable to them?
- What is the last time my position on a safety issue changed because of something a worker told me — and if I cannot remember, what does that tell me?

Common Field Traps

- Confusing the form of curiosity with the substance — asking questions in an interested tone while already holding a firm conclusion produces interrogation, not inquiry.
- Applying curiosity in comfortable situations and reverting to evaluation under pressure — the most important application of curiosity is precisely when the reflexive evaluative response is strongest.
- Using curiosity as a manipulation technique to lead workers to the conclusion you have already reached — this is quickly recognized and destroys trust.
- Treating curiosity as inefficiency — believing that the time spent understanding context is time taken away from correction. In most cases, understanding before correcting produces more durable change.

- Developing a personal practice of curiosity without building it into the crew's culture — one curious leader in a system designed for evaluation changes individual conversations but not the organizational information environment.

Prevention Practices

- Build one genuinely open question into every post-task debrief — a question you do not know the answer to and are genuinely interested in.
- Practice replacing your three most common reflexive evaluative responses with curious alternatives and use those alternatives consistently.
- Track the proportion of genuine inquiry questions versus evaluative questions in your safety conversations this week.
- When you observe behavior that seems unreasonable, develop the habit of asking 'what would have to be true for that to seem like a reasonable decision?' before responding.
- Build curiosity explicitly into your post-incident process: the first 15 minutes of any post-incident conversation should consist only of inquiry questions, no evaluative statements.

Connection to the 5 How's

The entire 5 How's framework is a structured expression of curiosity. 'How can this task fail?' is not a compliance question — it is a curiosity question. It asks leaders and workers to genuinely not know the answer and to investigate it together. Leaders who have developed genuine curiosity as a practice use the 5 How's as intended: as a thinking tool, not as a checklist.

Supervisor Toolbox Talk Prompt

Share this with your crew: 'I want to try something different today. I'm going to ask each of you one question about this task, and I genuinely don't know the answer. The question is: what is the most likely thing to go wrong on this task that we have not specifically planned for?' Then listen — not to evaluate, but to learn.

Chapter Summary

- Curiosity-first safety leadership produces better information, more honest accounts, and more accurate understanding of why things happen than evaluation-first responses.
- Genuine inquiry — questions asked without a predetermined answer — is perceptible to workers and creates a different quality of response than evaluative questioning.
- Developing curiosity as a practice requires replacing specific reflexive evaluative responses with genuine inquiry alternatives — this is a learnable skill that requires deliberate practice.
- One curious leader does not transform an evaluative organizational culture — building curiosity into the crew's shared norms requires consistent modeling and explicit expectation-setting.

Leader Action Checklist

[ ] Build one genuinely open question into your post-task debrief this week — something you do not know the answer to.

[ ] Identify your three most common reflexive evaluative responses in safety conversations and develop specific curious alternatives for each.

[ ] After your next safety conversation following an unsafe act, evaluate what proportion of your questions were genuine inquiry versus evaluative.

[ ] Practice the 'what would have to be true?' question when you observe behavior that seems unreasonable to you.

Chapter 20

BUILDING CULTURES WHERE PEOPLE THINK PREVENTIVELY

Leadership Issue

Safety culture is often described as if it is something an organization has or does not have — a fixed property that can be improved through programs and initiatives. In reality, culture is something an organization continuously creates through the accumulation of its practices, decisions, and leadership behaviors. A preventive safety culture is not established by announcing it — it is built through specific, consistent behaviors over time, especially under conditions of pressure and competing demands.

The Psychology Behind the Risk

Weick and Sutcliffe (2001) describe high-reliability organizations (HROs) — organizations that manage extreme hazard with consistently low incident rates — through five characteristics: preoccupation with failure, reluctance to simplify, sensitivity to operations, commitment to resilience, and deference to expertise. Of these, 'preoccupation with failure' is the most counterintuitive: HROs maintain active concern about what could go wrong even during periods of success. This is not pessimism — it is the disciplined practice of maintaining vigilance when success makes vigilance feel unnecessary.

Schein's research on organizational culture (1985) identifies assumptions as the deepest layer of culture — the beliefs that are so taken for granted that they are not consciously held or examined. In safety culture, the most important assumption is whether workers believe that reporting concerns, questioning plans, and voicing disagreement will be met with constructive response. This assumption is not formed by policies; it is formed by the accumulated evidence of actual leadership behavior over time.

Field Example

A crew begins every high-risk task by asking how it could fail, how controls will be verified, and what change would trigger a pause. This does not happen because a procedure requires it — it happens because it has become the crew's shared understanding of what good task preparation looks like. The question 'how could this fail?' is no longer asked because someone told them to ask it. It is asked because they believe it is the right question to ask before high-risk work.

Operational Mechanism

Culture is transmitted through modeling and reinforcement. Workers observe what leaders do, what leaders reward, and what leaders tolerate — and they build their behavioral norms around those observations. A culture of preventive thinking develops when leaders consistently model preventive questions, consistently reward early problem identification, and consistently respond constructively when workers surface concerns. The consistency over time is the mechanism; no single event creates or destroys a safety culture.

What Leaders Should Look For

- Workers who volunteer concerns and observations unprompted — not because they are required to, but because doing so is part of how they approach the work.
- Pre-task discussions where the crew naturally asks what could go wrong before someone in authority asks them to.
- Workers who stop the work when something unexpected happens, rather than continuing and adapting.
- A crew that uses learning language after problems rather than blame language — 'what did we miss?' rather than 'who messed up?'
- New employees who adopt preventive thinking practices within their first few months because the crew has transmitted them as norms.

Leadership Application

Culture building requires behavioral consistency at the leadership level over an extended period. The most powerful culture-building behaviors are the ones that occur under pressure — the moments when a leader could have taken the expedient route and instead took the safety-consistent one. These moments are remembered by the crew, discussed among the crew, and used as evidence about what the culture actually is.

Leaders building preventive culture should identify their three or four most important culture-building behaviors — the ones that are most visible to the crew and most indicative of their actual values — and practice them with particular consistency. The goal is not perfect execution of every safety behavior, but reliable demonstration of the behaviors that the crew uses to calibrate the culture.

Leadership Development Focus

Supervisors need to understand that they are culture carriers whether they intend to be or not. Every decision, every response to a concern, every incident reaction, every tolerance of a deviation is adding to the evidence pile that workers use to understand what the culture actually is. This means culture development is not a separate leadership activity — it is an interpretation of every leadership activity.

Practical Field Integration

Build a culture diagnostic into your regular review. Periodically ask: if I observed this crew for a week without them knowing who I was, what would I conclude their culture actually was — not their stated culture, but the beliefs about safety that their behavior reflects? The gap between the stated culture and the observable culture is the work.

Also build a crew culture conversation into your periodic team discussions: 'What do we actually believe around here about how safety works — not what we're supposed to say, but what our behavior shows we believe?' These conversations, when held in a psychologically safe environment, produce the most direct access to the cultural assumptions that drive behavior.

Leadership Questions

- If a new employee observed this crew for 30 days, what would they learn about how we actually approach safety — and is that what I want them to learn?
- What are the two or three most important behaviors I demonstrate consistently that teach the crew what this culture actually is?
- When was the last time the crew made a safety decision under pressure that reflected the culture I am trying to build — and did I recognize it explicitly?
- What is the gap between this crew's stated safety culture and their observable safety behavior — and what specific leadership behaviors are maintaining that gap?
- What does the crew believe happens to someone who surfaces a concern that slows the work — and is that belief accurate?

Common Field Traps

- Treating culture as something that can be installed through programs and initiatives rather than as something that accumulates through daily leadership behavior.
- Measuring culture by stated beliefs rather than by observed behavior — workers will describe a better culture than they live in.
- Expecting culture change to be visible quickly — genuine cultural change at the assumption level typically takes 18 to 36 months of consistent behavioral change.
- Building culture in calm periods without understanding that the crew forms its deepest cultural conclusions from the behavior they observe under pressure.
- Treating culture development as a separate leadership activity rather than as an interpretation of every leadership activity — culture is always being built or degraded.

Prevention Practices

- Identify the three or four culture-building behaviors that are most visible to the crew and practice them with particular consistency, especially under pressure.
- Build a culture diagnostic into your quarterly review: observe the crew as if you were an outside observer and describe the culture their behavior reflects.
- Conduct periodic crew culture conversations in a psychologically safe environment: 'What does our behavior show that we actually believe about safety?'
- Explicitly recognize crew members who model preventive thinking — stopping work for a concern, asking 'how could this fail?' before starting, volunteering a weak signal — as evidence that the culture is building.
- Track the consistency of your own culture-building behaviors over time — not just whether you modeled them in favorable conditions, but whether you maintained them when competing demands were highest.

Connection to the 5 How's

The 5 How's are a cultural artifact as much as a planning tool. In an organization where 'how can this fail?' is asked consistently, the question becomes part of the culture — an assumption about how good task preparation is done. The goal is not that the 5 How's are a required process; it is that they become the natural language of preventive thinking for everyone who does the work.

Supervisor Toolbox Talk Prompt

Ask your crew: 'Without referencing any policy or requirement — just based on what you've observed here over the last six months — what does the way we actually behave show that we believe about safety? And where does that differ from what we say?' Then listen. The gap between those two answers is the cultural work.

Chapter Summary

- Preventive safety culture is built through the accumulation of consistent leadership behavior over time, not through programs and initiatives — each decision, each response, each tolerance adds to the evidence workers use to understand what the culture actually is.
- The deepest cultural layer is the assumption about whether raising concerns will be met with constructive response — this assumption is not formed by policy but by the accumulated evidence of actual leadership behavior.
- Culture-building behaviors demonstrated under pressure are more powerful than behaviors demonstrated in favorable conditions — the crew forms its deepest conclusions from what they observe when the stakes are highest.
- The goal of preventive culture is a crew that asks 'how could this fail?' naturally, before being asked — because they believe it is the right question, not because a procedure requires it.

Leader Action Checklist

[ ] Identify your three most important culture-building behaviors and evaluate how consistently you demonstrated them in the last month, including under pressure.

[ ] Conduct a culture diagnostic this week: observe your crew as if you were an outside observer and describe the culture their behavior reflects.

[ ] Explicitly recognize one crew member this week for preventive thinking behavior — stopping work, asking the right question, surfacing a weak signal.

[ ] Hold a brief crew culture conversation: 'What does our behavior show that we actually believe about safety?' — and listen without evaluating.

Chapter 21

BEFORE THE MIND ACCEPTS THE RISK

Leadership Issue

This final chapter asks the question that all the preceding chapters have been building toward: what happens inside a person's mind in the period between first encountering a risk and accepting it as part of the work? That period — which may last seconds, days, months, or years — is where safety leadership has its greatest opportunity. Everything this volume has explored — normalization, pressure, silence, group behavior, shortcuts, drift, tone, trust — operates within that window. Leaders who understand the process can interrupt it. Leaders who do not understand it respond only to its outcomes.

The Psychology Behind the Risk

The psychology of risk acceptance is not a single event but a process. It begins with exposure: the worker encounters a hazard or risk condition. Initial response depends on the person's training, experience, and the context of first encounter — a hazard first encountered under supervision, with explicit instruction, produces different initial representation than one first encountered independently mid-task. Subsequent encounters either reinforce caution (when the hazard produces a near-consequence) or erode it (when repeated exposure produces no consequence).

Over time, if no consequence occurs and if the organizational environment provides no counter-signal, the brain re-categorizes the risk: from 'actively dangerous' to 'conditionally dangerous' to 'potentially dangerous' to 'probably fine.' This progression is the internal mechanism of all the phenomena this volume has described. Risk acceptance is not a decision — it is a drift, produced by cognitive, social, and organizational forces that operate largely outside of conscious awareness.

Field Example

By the time an injury occurs, the unsafe condition may have been seen, tolerated, and rationalized for months. The physical event is sudden, but the mental acceptance that made it possible developed slowly — through each day of exposure without consequence, through each supervisory walk-through without comment, through each crew conversation that treated the condition as unremarkable. The injury is the visible end of a long, invisible process.

Operational Mechanism

The process of risk acceptance can be interrupted at any point, but the earlier the interruption, the more effective it is. At first exposure, the worker's protective instincts are most active. After months of normalized exposure, the same interruption requires more effort and produces more resistance because it is working against an established mental model. This is why early response to weak signals is so much more efficient than late-stage intervention: prevention at the beginning of the process costs a fraction of what correction at the end requires.

What Leaders Should Look For

- The early stages: workers who express initial discomfort about a condition and then, over time, stop expressing it — the silence following early concern is a risk acceptance indicator.
- Vocabulary changes: workers who describe conditions that used to concern them in language that normalizes them — 'it's not ideal, but it's manageable.'
- The absence of first-time caution: new employees who do not show initial caution around established hazards because the crew's behavior has pre-normalized them.
- Leaders who were initially concerned about a condition and are no longer concerned despite no change in the condition — their acceptance is more dangerous than a worker's because it endorses the acceptance organizationally.

- The convergence of multiple risk acceptance processes simultaneously — when multiple conditions are simultaneously becoming more accepted, the system is in a particularly vulnerable state.

Leadership Application

The leader's role throughout this volume has been to interrupt the risk acceptance process — to create the counter-signal that the organizational environment must provide if the natural drift toward acceptance is to be resisted. That counter-signal takes many forms: the curious question that forces genuine engagement with a hazard, the visible pause that communicates that slowing down is acceptable, the response to a concern that communicates that raising concerns is valued, the baseline comparison that makes drift visible.

No leader can interrupt every risk acceptance process in every worker simultaneously. But leaders who understand the process can focus their limited time and attention on the points where intervention is most efficient: early in the exposure period, at the first sign of concern being withdrawn, and at moments when organizational pressure is accelerating the acceptance process.

Leadership Development Focus

The most important development implication of this chapter is that safety leadership is not primarily about managing hazards — it is about managing the human process of perceiving and responding to hazards. All the technical tools — JHAs, pre-task planning, inspection forms, safety observations — are valuable, but they are secondary to the leader's ability to maintain and restore the cognitive state that makes those tools work as intended: the state of genuine engagement with risk, not just procedural compliance with risk management tools.

Practical Field Integration

The integration of this entire volume comes down to a single standing practice: building opportunities for genuine engagement with risk into your regular operational rhythm, rather than relying on periodic formal processes. Pre-task conversations that ask real questions. Safety walks that look for what has changed rather than confirming that nothing has. Post-task reviews that capture what the crew learned. Coaching conversations that build understanding rather than only assigning consequence. These practices, done consistently and honestly, interrupt the risk acceptance process before it produces the event that makes it visible.

This is the work of safety leadership. Not the paperwork. Not the inspections. Not the metrics. The constant, patient, consistent work of keeping human engagement with risk genuine in environments where every natural force pushes toward acceptance.

Leadership Questions

- Where in my work area are multiple risk acceptance processes occurring simultaneously — and what does that convergence tell me about the system's current vulnerability?
- Which workers first expressed concern about a condition and have since stopped expressing it — and what produced that transition?
- Where are the early-stage risk acceptance processes happening right now — the conditions that workers are currently uncomfortable with but have not yet fully normalized?
- What organizational signals am I sending that are accelerating risk acceptance — and which ones am I sending that are decelerating it?
- If I could only do one thing from all twenty-one chapters to improve safety outcomes in this operation, what would it be — and am I doing it?

Common Field Traps

- Focusing safety leadership effort on the endpoint of the risk acceptance process — the incident — rather than on the process that produced it.

- Treating the risk acceptance process as the worker's problem rather than as a joint product of the worker, the organizational environment, and the leadership signals they receive.
- Using periodic formal safety processes (audits, inspections) as the primary intervention tool rather than building genuine engagement into the daily operational rhythm.
- Concluding that when the technical controls are in place, the human side of safety management is adequately addressed.
- Treating this volume's concepts as separate topics rather than as descriptions of the same process viewed from different angles — they are all aspects of how humans come to accept risks they should not accept.

Prevention Practices

- Build a standing practice of early-stage risk acceptance identification: ask periodically which workers used to express concern about a condition and no longer do.
- Create a personal leadership inventory from this volume: identify the two chapters whose concepts are most active in your current work environment and apply them specifically.
- Build a complete operational rhythm around the themes in this volume: pre-task questions that surface genuine engagement, observations that look for drift, post-task reviews that build learning, coaching conversations that build understanding.
- Maintain the discipline of baseline comparison: regularly measuring current conditions and behaviors against documented standards, not against recent practice.
- Commit to the long game: safety culture and individual risk perception change slowly and require consistent leadership behavior over months and years, not periodic intensive efforts.

Connection to the 5 How's

The 5 How's are the practical expression of everything this volume has described. They interrupt the risk acceptance process at the task level — by asking, before every significant task, how it could fail and how failure will be prevented. Used consistently and honestly, they are not just a planning tool. They are a practice of genuine engagement with risk in an environment where every natural force pushes toward acceptance.

Supervisor Toolbox Talk Prompt

End with this: 'We've covered a lot in this series about why people accept risks they shouldn't. Today I want to ask you directly: what is the one thing in our daily work that you have become more comfortable with over time — more comfortable than the actual risk level justifies? What's the one thing that used to concern you more than it does now?' The answer to that question is where the work is.

Chapter Summary

- Risk acceptance is not a decision but a drift — a gradual psychological process driven by repeated exposure without consequence, organizational signals that normalize conditions, and the natural reduction of initial protective instincts.
- The risk acceptance process can be interrupted at any point, but early interruption is far more efficient than late-stage correction — this is the fundamental argument for preventive safety leadership.
- All the concepts in this volume — normalization, pressure, silence, shortcuts, group behavior, drift, tone, trust — are descriptions of the same process viewed from different angles: how humans come to accept risks they should not accept.
- Safety leadership is not primarily about managing hazards. It is about managing the human process of perceiving and responding to hazards — and that process requires consistent, patient, genuine engagement, not periodic formal intervention.

Leader Action Checklist

[ ] Identify where the earliest-stage risk acceptance processes are currently occurring in your work area — conditions workers are currently uncomfortable with but have not yet fully normalized.

[ ] Select the two chapters from this volume whose concepts are most actively present in your current work environment and create a specific action plan for each.

[ ] Build a complete operational rhythm from the practices in this volume: pre-task questions, observation focus, post-task review, and coaching conversation practice.

[ ] Commit to one 90-day consistent practice from this volume — not a program, not a one-time effort, but a daily behavioral commitment — and evaluate the result.

APPENDIX A — PSYCHOLOGICAL WARNING SIGNS IN OPERATIONAL ENVIRONMENTS

The following indicators suggest that psychological conditions — stress, fatigue, normalization, fear, or fixation — may be affecting behavior and safety outcomes in your work environment.

Communication Changes

- Shortened planning discussions without corresponding reduction in task complexity
- Assumption-based briefings replacing verification-based ones
- Reduced questioning before high-risk tasks
- Employees who were previously vocal becoming consistently quiet

Behavioral Indicators

- Task completion pace inconsistent with procedure timelines
- Verification steps completed without visible pause or engagement
- Workers who startle at conditions in their own work area
- Protective equipment worn correctly at task start but incorrectly by mid-task

Crew Dynamic Signals

- Unanimous agreement in pre-task meetings without apparent discussion
- New employees adopting crew-specific practices within the first two weeks
- No visible reaction to known hazards from experienced workers
- Concerns raised informally but not formally reported

Leadership Signals

- Post-incident conversations that end with assigned consequence but no documented system learning

- Safety observations that consistently find the same conditions without producing systemic correction
- Reporting trend decline following disciplinary actions
- Workers who preface concerns with 'I'm probably wrong, but...'

APPENDIX B — LEADERSHIP CONVERSATION EXAMPLES

The following examples demonstrate the difference between evaluation-first and curiosity-first leadership responses in common safety leadership situations.

After an Unsafe Act

- Evaluation-first: 'You know the procedure. Why didn't you follow it?'
- Curiosity-first: 'Walk me through what you were seeing at the time. What made that approach seem like the right call?'

After a Near-Miss

- Evaluation-first: 'Who was responsible for the barricade?'
- Curiosity-first: 'Let's walk through the sequence together. I want to understand what conditions came together to create that moment.'

Before a High-Risk Task

- Evaluation-first: 'Everyone know what they're doing? Good. Let's go.'
- Curiosity-first: 'Before we start — what's the one thing about this task that could most likely go wrong today? And what's our specific plan for that?'

During a Toolbox Talk

- Evaluation-first: 'Everybody read the safety card? Sign here.'
- Curiosity-first: 'I want to hear from each person individually — what's your biggest concern about this task based on conditions right now?'

APPENDIX C – PSYCHOLOGICAL TRIGGERS THAT INFLUENCE UNSAFE DECISIONS

Safety decisions are influenced by psychological triggers that operate outside of conscious awareness. Understanding these triggers helps leaders identify conditions that increase risk before a decision is made.

Cognitive Triggers

- Familiarity bias: hazards perceived as less dangerous because they have not recently produced harm
- Outcome bias: evaluating the quality of a decision by its result rather than the conditions in which it was made
- Confirmation bias: looking for evidence that conditions are acceptable rather than evidence that they are not
- Optimism bias: believing that negative outcomes are less likely to occur to oneself than to others

Social Triggers

- Social proof: adopting the behavior of the group as implicit guidance on what is acceptable
- Conformity pressure: changing or withholding a position to avoid standing out from group consensus
- Authority compliance: executing a plan one believes is inadequate because a person in authority approved it
- Diffusion of responsibility: assuming someone else will address a concern because others are present

Environmental Triggers

- Time pressure: reducing the cognitive resources allocated to hazard assessment when schedule demands are high
- Fatigue: degrading executive function while leaving routine procedural execution relatively intact
- High workload: narrowing attentional focus in ways that reduce peripheral hazard awareness

- Novel situations: increasing cognitive load in ways that reduce the capacity for hazard assessment

APPENDIX D — CREW COMMUNICATION INDICATORS

Communication quality is one of the most sensitive early indicators of safety system health. The following indicators can be used to assess communication quality in your work environment.

High-Quality Communication Indicators

- Crew members ask clarifying questions before beginning high-risk tasks
- Concerns are raised before work starts rather than after it finishes
- Workers acknowledge uncertainty explicitly: 'I'm not sure about this part'
- Plans are challenged by crew members when conditions change
- Communication includes explicit verification of shared understanding: 'So we all agree that...'

Communication Quality Decline Indicators

- Pre-task discussions becoming consistently shorter without corresponding task simplification
- Workers completing each other's sentences or assuming shared understanding without verifying it
- Questions asked after tasks are completed that should have been asked before they started
- Communication defaulting to abbreviations and shorthand that hide ambiguity
- A reduction in the number of people who actively participate in pre-task discussions

APPENDIX E — PREVENTIVE OBSERVATION GUIDE

Use this guide to structure safety observations that look for early psychological and behavioral indicators rather than only physical hazard conditions.

Before the Task

- Ask a specific question about what could fail and listen for depth: do workers identify specific current conditions or give generic answers?
- Observe how the crew interacts during planning: are questions welcomed, is there genuine discussion, does everyone participate?
- Note whether the plan addresses what has changed since the last time this task was performed

During the Task

- Observe communication quality: are workers verifying shared understanding or assuming it?
- Note the pace of verification steps: are they being completed as genuine checks or as formalities?
- Watch for task fixation indicators: workers who have stopped scanning their environment while executing a complex step

After the Task

- Ask: what did you learn about this task that you did not know before you started?
- Ask: was there anything during this task that did not go exactly as planned?
- Note whether the crew's description of how the task went matches what you observed during it

APPENDIX F — LEADERSHIP REFLECTION WORKSHEETS

Use these reflection questions to build your own preventive safety leadership practice.

Weekly Reflection

- What condition in my work area did I notice this week that I had not been actively seeing?
- What did my behavior communicate this week about the relative priority of safety and production?
- What concern was raised this week and what did my response communicate about whether raising concerns is valued?
- What am I currently tolerating that I would not have tolerated 12 months ago?

Monthly Reflection

- What is the trend in near-miss and concern reporting this month compared to last month — and what is causing any change?
- What normalized condition exists in my work area that an outside observer would identify as concerning?
- What crew behavior under pressure best reflects the safety culture I am trying to build — and what most undermines it?
- Where is the gap between my stated safety culture and my crew's observable safety behavior?

After Any Safety Event

- What conditions contributed to this outcome — not just the immediate cause but the system conditions that made the behavior feel reasonable?
- What did our response to this event communicate to the workforce about what happens when safety information is shared?
- What system change would make the safer choice easier in similar future conditions?

- What would I do differently if I knew six months ago what I know now?

APPENDIX G — THE PSYCHOLOGY OF SAFETY ANCHOR FRAMEWORK

The Anchor Framework summarizes the core concepts of this volume as a practical reference for leaders.

The Five Psychological Forces

- Normalization: repeated exposure without consequence reduces the perceived danger of established hazards
- Pressure: schedule, social, and authority pressure shift the relative weight of competing priorities
- Silence: fear of consequences and belief that reporting is futile both suppress the safety communication channel
- Fatigue: cognitive degradation that reduces error detection and hazard assessment capacity
- Drift: the gradual accumulation of individually reasonable deviations that collectively represent dangerous departure from standard

The Four Leadership Responses

- Interrupt normalization: create regular re-sensitization opportunities for familiar hazards
- Counter pressure: send explicit behavioral signals that pausing for safety is genuinely acceptable
- Build voice: close the loop on every concern and create visible evidence that reporting produces response
- Maintain standards: respond to the first deviation, compare current practice to documented baseline, and resist rationalization of drift

The Prevention Mindset

- Ask how before asking why: examine conditions before examining individuals
- Look for the weak signal before it becomes a strong one
- Measure current practice against documented standard, not against recent history

- Build genuine curiosity as a leadership posture: ask questions you do not already know the answer to

APPENDIX H — SUPERVISOR COACHING GUIDE FOR HUMAN PERFORMANCE

This guide provides a structured approach for coaching supervisors in human performance concepts.

Coaching Session Structure

- Open with a specific field observation: 'I noticed that [specific behavior or condition] in [specific situation]'
- Ask a genuine inquiry question: 'Help me understand your perspective on that situation'
- Connect to a human performance concept from this volume without naming it as a theory
- Develop a specific behavioral practice together: 'What would you do differently next time?'
- Close with a follow-up commitment: 'I'll check in with you in two weeks on this'

Coaching Topics by Volume Chapter

- Ch 1-3: Normalization and familiarity — use fresh eyes observation as the coaching tool
- Ch 4-5: Pressure and silence — use crew reporting trend as the coaching prompt
- Ch 6-7: Fatigue and fixation — use end-of-shift behavioral observation as the coaching tool
- Ch 8-10: Communication and group dynamics — use pre-task discussion quality as the coaching prompt
- Ch 11-14: Tone, coaching, trust, and normalization of deviance — use trust temperature check as the coaching tool
- Ch 15-21: EI, shortcuts, signals, drift, curiosity, culture, risk acceptance — use baseline comparison as the coaching prompt

APPENDIX I — TRAINING MODULE OUTLINE

This outline supports conversion of Volume I content into a structured training program for supervisor development.

Module 1: Why Incidents Happen to Good People (Chapters 1-3)

- Learning objective: Participants can explain three psychological mechanisms that contribute to unsafe decisions by capable workers
- Key concepts: System conditions, hindsight bias, habituation, familiarity bias
- Activity: Fresh eyes observation exercise — identify what normalization has made invisible
- Assessment: Case analysis using a provided incident scenario

Module 2: How Pressure and Silence Create Hidden Risk (Chapters 4-5)

- Learning objective: Participants can identify and counter implicit signals that suppress safe behavior
- Key concepts: Production pressure, social pressure, psychological safety, learned silence
- Activity: Implicit signal audit — review own communication behaviors over the past week
- Assessment: Debrief with a peer on what signals they observed in each other's behavior

Module 3: Fatigue, Fixation, and Cognitive Risk (Chapters 6-7)

- Learning objective: Participants can recognize cognitive fatigue and task fixation in field conditions
- Key concepts: Cognitive fatigue, metacognition, inattentional blindness, role designation
- Activity: Shift observation practice — end-of-shift behavioral comparison to start-of-shift baseline

- Assessment: Develop a fixation management plan for one high-focus task in their work area

Module 4: Leadership Tone, Coaching, and Trust (Chapters 8-14)

- Learning objective: Participants can describe the specific behaviors that build vs. erode trust and voice
- Key concepts: Emotional contagion, learned helplessness, conformity, normalization of deviance
- Activity: Trust temperature check — conduct a private conversation with a crew member
- Assessment: Develop a personal trust behavior standard with three specific commitments

Module 5: Preventive Safety Leadership (Chapters 15-21)

- Learning objective: Participants can apply at least three preventive leadership practices in their current work environment
- Key concepts: Emotional intelligence, shortcut rationalization, weak signals, drift, curiosity, culture
- Activity: 90-day leadership practice commitment — select and document one behavioral commitment
- Assessment: Peer coaching session using the 5 How's framework applied to a real current task

CONCLUSION

The twenty-one chapters of this volume describe a single phenomenon from twenty-one angles: the process by which capable people come to accept risks they should not accept, in environments that have gradually taught them that those risks are reasonable.

That process is not the product of carelessness, bad attitude, or inadequate training. It is the product of how human beings perceive, adapt to, and respond to the environments they work in every day. It is produced by organizational pressure, by the silence that follows dismissed concerns, by the fatigue that no one names, by the group dynamics that replace individual judgment, and by the leadership behavior that normalizes what should alarm.

The work of safety leadership is not to eliminate human adaptability — that is neither possible nor desirable. It is to create and maintain the conditions under which adaptive human behavior points toward safety rather than away from it. That requires understanding the psychology. It requires developing the leadership skills. And it requires the patience and consistency to practice those skills even when the pressure to take shortcuts is highest.

The remaining volumes in this series build on what this volume has established. Volume II develops the coaching skills that put these concepts into practice with the people you lead. Volume III introduces the 5 How's framework as a practical preventive analysis tool for field leaders. Volume IV integrates preventive and investigative analysis into a complete leadership reference. Later volumes extend the work into safety finance, field leadership, and practical supervisor tools.

The work you are doing matters. The incidents that do not happen are invisible — no one knows they were prevented, no one files a report, no one attends the review. But they are the measure of this work. Every conversation that surfaced a concern before it became an event, every pause that interrupted a drift toward exposure, every question that made risk visible before it became harm — those are what this series is designed to support.

Keep asking how before you ask why. Keep looking for the early signal. Keep building the conditions in which the people you lead believe that speaking up is worth it. That is the work.

REFERENCES

Asch, S. E. (1951). Effects of group pressure upon the modification and distortion of judgments. In H. Guetzkow (Ed.), Groups, leadership, and men. Carnegie Press.

Baumeister, R. F., & Leary, M. R. (1995). The need to belong: Desire for interpersonal attachments as a fundamental human motivation. Psychological Bulletin, 117(3), 497–529.

Dekker, S. (2006). The field guide to understanding human error. Ashgate.

Dekker, S. (2011). Drift into failure: From hunting broken components to understanding complex systems. Ashgate.

Edmondson, A. (1999). Psychological safety and learning behavior in work teams. Administrative Science Quarterly, 44(2), 350–383.

Goleman, D. (1995). Emotional intelligence: Why it can matter more than IQ. Bantam Books.

Green, D. M., & Swets, J. A. (1966). Signal detection theory and psychophysics. Wiley.

Hollnagel, E. (2014). Safety-I and Safety-II: The past and future of safety management. Ashgate.

Kahneman, D. (2011). Thinking, fast and slow. Farrar, Straus and Giroux.

Latané, B., & Darley, J. M. (1970). The unresponsive bystander: Why doesn't he help? Appleton-Century-Crofts.

LeDoux, J. (1996). The emotional brain: The mysterious underpinnings of emotional life. Simon & Schuster.

Mayer, R. C., Davis, J. H., & Schoorman, F. D. (1995). An integrative model of organizational trust. Academy of Management Review, 20(3), 709–734.

Morrison, E. W., & Milliken, F. J. (2000). Organizational silence: A barrier to change and development in a pluralistic world. Academy of Management Review, 25(4), 706–725.

Rasmussen, J. (1997). Risk management in a dynamic society: A modelling problem. Safety Science, 27(2–3), 183–213.

Reason, J. (1990). Human error. Cambridge University Press.

Reason, J. (1997). Managing the risks of organizational accidents. Ashgate.

Schein, E. H. (1985). Organizational culture and leadership. Jossey-Bass.

Seligman, M. E. P. (1972). Learned helplessness. Annual Review of Medicine, 23(1), 407–412.

Simons, D. J., & Chabris, C. F. (1999). Gorillas in our midst: Sustained inattentional blindness for dynamic events. Perception, 28(9), 1059–1074.

Vaughan, D. (1996). The Challenger launch decision: Risky technology, culture, and deviance at NASA. University of Chicago Press.

Weick, K. E., & Sutcliffe, K. M. (2001). Managing the unexpected: Assuring high performance in an age of complexity. Jossey-Bass.

Williamson, A. M., & Feyer, A. M. (2000). Moderate sleep deprivation produces impairments in cognitive and motor performance equivalent to legally prescribed levels of alcohol intoxication. Occupational and Environmental Medicine, 57(10), 649–655.

Zohar, D. (2002). The effects of leadership dimensions, safety climate, and assigned priorities on minor injuries in work groups. Journal of Organizational Behavior, 23(1), 75–92.

ABOUT THE AUTHOR

James Dye is a safety professional, military veteran, and operational safety leader with extensive experience in high-hazard environments. His work focuses on the human side of safety — the behavioral, psychological, and organizational factors that determine whether safety systems work as intended or fail in the field.

Drawing on his military background and years of operational safety leadership, James developed the Professional Safety Leadership Series to address a consistent gap in safety education: most safety training focuses on what to do after something goes wrong. This series focuses on what to understand, observe, and do before failure occurs.

The series reflects James's conviction that the most effective safety leaders are not those who enforce the most rules, but those who understand most clearly why people do what they do — and who use that understanding to build environments in which the safe choice is also the natural one.

www.ingramcontent.com/pod-product-compliance
Lightning Source LLC
LaVergne TN
LVHW022223200926
848481LV00006B/2087